YESTERDAY AND TODAY

THE HOLY LAND

LITHOGRAPHS BY DAVID ROBERTS

WHITE STAR
PUBLISHERS

Yaffa, ancient Joppa.

April 16 1839.

David Roberts R.A.

Isle of Graie Gulf of Akabah — Arabia Petraea, Feby 27th 1839

4

David Roberts R. A

Ruins of the Circular Temple of the Temple of Baalbec

YESTERDAY AND TODAY
THE HOLY LAND

LITHOGRAPHS BY DAVID ROBERTS

Texts by
Fabio Bourbon

Photographs by
Antonio Attini

Design by
Patrizia Balocco Lovisetti

Translation by
Antony Shugaar

CONTENTS

Thanks are due to the following people
for their valuable contributions to this book:
Dr. Shefer, Tourism Office of Israel;
Oded Ben-Hur, Israeli Embassy in Rome.

Special thanks to:
Eliana Sachar, Maria Luisa Gurgo, Davide Silvera.

© 1994, 2004 White Star S.r.l.
Via Candido Sassone, 22/24
13100 Vercelli, Italy
www.whitestar.it

ISBN 88-544-000-2
REPRINTS:
 3456 08 07 06 05 04

Printed in Singapore

2-3 *Jaffa, looking south.*

4-5 *Island of Graia, Gulf of Aqaba.*

6-7 *Baalbec, portion of the eastern portico.*

8-9 *The gate of Damascus.*

INTRODUCTION

Clearly, David Roberts was a man of character, as well as an original and expressive artist. Born into a poor and humble family, on the outskirts of Edinburgh, Roberts successfully rose above his humble origins, winning recognition and fame.

His outstanding views of the Imperial Forum in Rome, or of Gothic cathedrals in the Iberian Peninsula, his impressive monumental views of the temples of the pharaohs in the Nile Valley, his sketches of his native Scotland - all are familiar to art experts and art lovers. Untrained connoisseurs readily recognize his style, almost instinctively. The overriding sensation of sober and finely proportioned grandeur that permeates every piece of work by David Roberts, the unmistakable descriptive attention to detail that infuses even the humblest of subjects with dignity - note the portraits of peasants. All of these qualities have exerted a great and immediate influence upon the imagination of the public.

Let it come as no surprise then that reproductions of his work have been used, especially in this century, to illustrate just about everything: from run-of-the-mill tourist guides to glossy travel posters.

During Roberts's lifetime he enjoyed a vast circle of private clients who commissioned extensively, and a great many collectors who traded in his work. Since then, interest has grown steadily and never flagged. Although versatile and prolific, ranging widely in his choice of subjects, David Roberts nowadays owes much of his fame and popularity to his lithographs of the Middle East. In particular, the fruit of his wanderings in the Holy Land, which during Roberts's lifetime won him great and lasting acclaim, is now considered to be a masterpiece and has survived the test of time and fashion. This volume contains the one hundred twenty-three lithographs realized from the sketches that Roberts executed during his voyage through the Sinai Peninsula to Jerusalem and, finally, to the spectacular city of Baalbec.

The illustrations, large in format, are reproduced from the first edition, in three volumes, published in London between 1842 and 1849 by Francis Graham Moon with the original title of "The Holy Land, Syria, Idumea, Egypt, Nubia." That edition is now among the collections of the Victoria and Albert Museum. Clearly, given the format of this edition, the sections on Egypt and Nubia are not included here. The most important new development in this edition of the work is that the lithographs are shown, we believe for the first time, in strict chronological order beginning with Roberts's arrival in Suez on the 10th of February 1839 and running all the way through to his departure from Baalbec, which took place on the 8th of May of the same year. It has thus become necessary to resolve many of the considerable problems in the dating of each and in its precise place in this work. The previous editions have always emphasized the purely visual aspects of the creations of this artist, and have done so to the detriment of an accurate reflection of the historical and geographical details involved, so that the illustrations have been arranged in various ways by various publishers; in some cases by geographical zone, in other cases by type of subject, and in yet other cases by purely esthetic and chromatic affinities. Roberts himself tended not to pay too much attention to these matters, and it should also be kept in mind that the publication of his works was a process that stretched out over eight years, a length of time that necessarily generated a number of "oversights." The length of time involved in publication certainly exacerbated the problems in chronology since some of the lithographs - which were executed by the Belgian plate maker Louis Haghe, working on the sketches that Roberts made during his travels - bear no dates, while a great many others have inaccurate dates. An example: plate 48 in this edition bears the indication "19th April 1841," in the margin. This is necessarily an

This portrait of David Roberts in oriental garb was painted by Robert Scott Launder in 1840. (Reproduced here by kind permission of the Scottish National Portrait Gallery)

erroneous date because by that time Roberts had already been back in London for twenty-one months. In some cases, these inaccuracies can be attributed to the artist's momentary distraction; in other cases, to a careless oversight on the part of Louis Haghe who, it seems logical to guess, must have been tempted in more than one instance to "complete" his plates with chronological notations, thus causing glaring contradictions with the information contained in Roberts's travel journal. The fact that the handwriting of the notes to a number of plates should be different from the handwriting found elsewhere, along with the significant detail that in certain cases Haghe placed his own signature alongside that of Roberts (one may see this on the frontispiece of the first chapter, as well as on plates 26, 30, and 35), persuades us we may be right; i.e. that the plates passed through a great many different hands. Other liberties that we have ventured to take include the following: we have split up the route that Roberts took into three separate phases, which are indicated on the map shown here in three different colors that correspond to the three different chapters. It is no accident that each of the chapters opens with one of the original frontispieces from the three volumes of the first edition, portraying the most intriguing places that

Roberts visited: Petra, Jerusalem, and Baalbec. It is, moreover, not out of line to suggest that for the English artist, the three trips from Suez to Jerusalem - with his exploration of the mythical capital of the Nabateans, his tour of the Holy City and descent to the Jordan River, and, lastly, the trip from Jerusalem to the ancient Heliopolis - constitute three different emotional experiences. The first edition was in effect split up into three different volumes. We have arranged them so as to provide a more precise visual chronicle of the trip. We should, however, point out that the original edition overseen by Roberts began with lithographs of Jerusalem, and that it did not include his travel diary, the well-known journal that proved to be so useful in the work done on this present edition: the journal, in fact, has allowed us to amend gaps in the chronology so that the sequence of pictures presented here is as close as possible to the actual travel experiences that Roberts himself enjoyed. If, therefore, we have not been entirely faithful to the first edition, we believe that we have at least restored to this remarkable artistic enterprise that degree of "legibility" which for many years was entirely lacking. We have also chosen to provide a commentary to each plate with brief historic and geographic notations in order to provide a narrative of the

episodes described and shown by Roberts himself. In each case, with a view to philological accuracy, we have chosen to accompany many of the illustrations with major excerpts from Roberts's journal, giving some indication of the English artist's gifts for brevity and description. The reader may notice that those commentaries that emphasize the historical background of the places visited by Roberts tend to emphasize the distant past rather than the recent past and the present. We want this to be a book describing the travels of a man living in the nineteenth century, and not an atlas of the modern Middle East. A bridge spanning the distance between past and present is offered by the splendid photographs taken by Antonio Attini, a young photojournalist who retraced the voyage of David Roberts, taking photographs that correspond with the lithographs. This unusual mingling of such radically different pictures is particularly informative regarding the inexorable results of the passage of time. These photographs have no commentary: the reader can draw his or her own conclusions, or imagine a modern trip through what is certainly one of the most appealing and perhaps mysterious regions in the world. Before such eloquence, we shall leave the pictures to speak for themselves.

Fabio Bourbon

In this map, which was also published in the first edition of "The Holy Land," printed by Francis Graham Moon, we can see the route that David Roberts followed. The three colors correspond to the chapters of this volume.

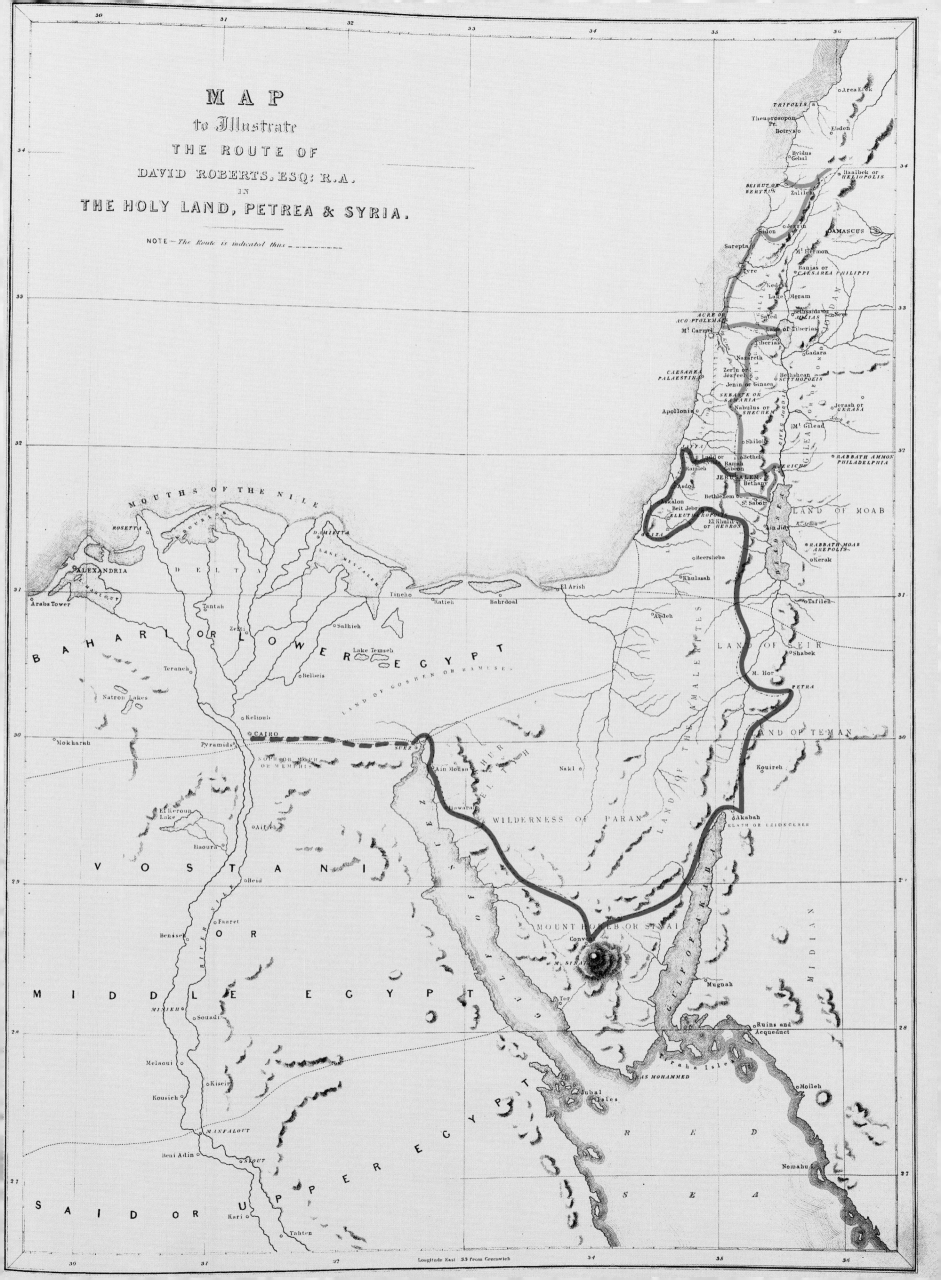

MAP
to Illustrate
THE ROUTE OF
DAVID ROBERTS, ESQ. R.A.
IN
THE HOLY LAND, PETREA & SYRIA.

NOTE.—The Route is indicated thus ——————

LIST OF PLATES

DAVID ROBERTS'S JOURNEY THROUGH THE HOLY LAND HAS BEEN SUPPORTED AND HELPED BY SEVERAL PEOPLE AND
AUTHORITIES, AMONG WHICH WE WOULD LIKE TO REMEMBER:

HER ROYAL HIGHNESS THE QUEEN
HER MAJESTY ADELAIDE, THE QUEEN DOWAGER.
HIS IMPERIAL MAJESTY THE EMPEROR OF ALL RUSSIAS.
HIS IMPERIAL MAJESTY THE EMPEROR OF AUSTRIA.
HIS MAJESTY THE KING OF FRANCE.
HIS MAJESTY THE KING OF PRUSSIA.
HIS MAJESTY THE KING OF BAVARIA.
HIS HIGHNESS MEHEMET ALI, PASHA OF EGYPT.
HIS GRACE THE LORD ARCHBISHOP OF CANTERBURY.
HIS GRACE THE LORD ARCHBISHOP OF YORK.
THE RIGHT HONORABLE LORD WHARNCLIFFE, LORD PRESIDENT OF THE COUNCIL.
HIS SERENE HIGHNESS PRINCE ESTERHAZE.
HIS GRACE THE DUKE OF WELLINGTON, CHANCELLOR OF THE UNIVERSITY OF OXFORD.
HIS GRACE THE DUKE OF NORTHUMBERLAND, CHANCELLOR OF THE UNIVERSITY OF CAMBRIDGE.
THE RIGHT HONORABLE SIR ROBERT PEEL, BART., M.P., FIRST LORD OF THE TREASURY.
THE HONORABLE EAST INDIA COMPANY.

BIOGRAPHY OF DAVID ROBERTS

The son of a cobbler, David Roberts was born on the 24th of October 1796 in Stockbridge, not far from Edinburgh. Although the environment in which Roberts grew up was far from refined or cultivated, his own natural artistic talent showed itself early. His mother encouraged the young David Roberts, describing her native town, St. Andrews, where the ruins of a well-known cathedral and a vast monastery still stood. Impressed by the colorful posters that announced the arrival of a travelling circus, young David covered the walls of the kitchen with long lines of animals and circus figures, lined with considerable expertise in red chalk. It was then that his curiosity began to be aroused by the idea of distant lands; it was then that his great thirst for travel and adventure was first awakened. While still a young a boy, he visited every castle and ruin in the surrounding countryside, sketching everything from almost every angle imaginable. Nonetheless, the desperate economic conditions of his family precluded a thorough, professional artistic education, aside from a seven-year apprenticeship with a local decorator named Gavin Beugo, whose name had been given to the Roberts family by the director of the Trustees Academy of Edinburgh. In all likelihood, Beugo, a strict and even authoritarian master, was the only source of the fundamentals of artistic technique; the young Roberts was and basically remained a brilliantly self-taught artist. From this period dates a curious anecdote that provides ample confirmation of the artist's innate qualities. Beugo had given his young apprentice a one-pound banknote with which to pay a supplier. The supplier, however, was out when Roberts arrived, and while waiting for him, Roberts had all the time he needed to make a perfect copy of the banknote, probably never having held one in his hands before. A short time later, Roberts's mother was putting some order in her son's collection of drawings; she saw the copy of the banknote and was shocked at the thought that she might have raised a young thief, before realizing that it was merely a copy.

In 1815, Roberts moved to Perth where he had his first professional job as a paid decorator. He returned to Edinburgh at the age of nineteen, found work as an assistant set designer in a small, second-run theater called the Pantheon. Later on, he wrote that this was the crowning attainment of his fondest ambitions, because this close contact with the fantastic world of the theater allowed his imagination to soar toward other, distant lands; while working upon a production of "Ali Baba and the Forty Thieves," he felt that he had become familiar with Baghdad, with its minarets and enchanted nights. For the moment, however, he had not the slightest glimmering of his future travels in the Middle East. In 1819 he became the official painter of the Royal Theatre in Glasgow, and later held the same position at the Royal Theatre in Edinburgh. David Roberts married Margaret McLachlan in 1820, but it soon became clear that this was an unfortunate match, and the couple separated after a couple of years. Nonetheless, Roberts was always a devoted and caring father to his only daughter, Christine. Roberts and his daughter remained in constant and affectionate contact, and in later years Christine was in charge of organizing her father's work and copying his travel journals. Toward the end of 1821 his reputation grew to the point that he was hired by the Drury Lane Theatre in London, along with his good friend Clarkson Stanfield. In 1824, Roberts's first oil painting, a view of Dryburgh, was shown at the British Institution; two years later Roberts debuted at the prestigious Covent Garden. In this same period of time, his "View of the Cathedral of Rouen" was shown at the Royal Academy, and his art began to receive high critical praise for its subtlety and magnificence. Even the Times of London spoke

David Roberts, as shown in the first edition of "The Holy Land."

highly of his work. In the meanwhile, Roberts had been involved in the foundation of the Society of British Artists, and was elected chairman of the same in 1831. Despite his rapidly growing commitments due to the enthusiastic response of private clients, Roberts had many opportunities to travel in Europe during the early years of his career, bringing back numerous sketches that would later serve as models for his paintings. Aside from his celebrated views of places in France, Germany, and the Netherlands, he did a great many sketches of his native land, and during his frequent visits to his parents, he toured all of the major monuments in Scotland, taking inspiration for some of his finest works. Among other things, during these explorations he completed a remarkable series of engravings; unfortunately, after the first edition sold out, they were not reprinted. Encouraged by the increasingly positive response of the public, Roberts progressively abandoned his work as a stage designer and turned to the far more lucrative field of studio painting. At the advice of his friend Wilkie, Roberts decided to travel to Spain, a land that was then little known, which proved to be a fertile source of inspiration for his creative drive. Before leaving England, he completed a series of works that Sir Edward Bulwer-Lytton

had commissioned him to do, entitled "Pilgrims of the Rhine." During the journey, which lasted almost two years, Roberts was able to visit almost all of the major cities in Spain, including Madrid, Toledo, Granada, Malaga, Seville, and Gibraltar. In the meanwhile, he tirelessly sketched ruins and monuments dating from a vast a range of eras, with particular attention to Moorish art and the local flamboyant Gothic. In 1837, a selection of these sketches was published, with the title of "Picturesque Sketches of Spain." After just two months, a considerable number of copies - twelve hundred - had been sold, and Roberts would have been a rich man had it not been for the larcenous ways of the publisher. Roberts was accepted as an associate of the Royal Academy in 1838; nonetheless, during the same period, he was preparing to achieve one of the dreams of his youth. With the money he had saved during his Spanish travels, he was preparing to set off on a journey to the places that were settings for the events recorded in the Bible. This journey was to make him famous, ensuring his name a place in history. For many years he had minutely recorded all the information available concerning the customs and everyday life, and the political and social situation in Egypt, Palestine, and Syria. (It should be noted that during this era, Syria was the name given to the enormous territory between the Mediterranean and the Euphrates, between Asia Minor in the north and the Arabian Peninsula and Egypt to the south). Thanks to his influential friends, Roberts was successful in obtaining a number of letters of introduction from the Ministry for Foreign Affairs, addressed to the general consuls in Egypt and Syria. In August 1838, he set out for Paris, travelling down the Rhône Valley to Marseilles, where he arrived on the 11th of September. Here he took passage on a steamer heading for Civitavecchia. In his journal, which became famous as "David Roberts's Journal," he expressed his regret at being so close to Rome without being able to visit the Eternal City. Six days later, he was on Malta, and then in the Cyclades, a group of Greek islands in the southern Aegean. At the end of September, he finally docked in the port of Alexandria. For three months he sailed up the Nile, on board a vessel that he had rented only after considerable difficulty; he succeeded in visiting all of the major archeological sites in the region and ventured as far south as Nubia and Abu Simbel. Toward the end of this exploration, he lost all of the sketches and paintings he had produced thus far on his journey, but managed to recover them in an adventuresome fashion. On the 21st of December, Roberts was once again in Cairo with

more than a hundred sketches and paintings. He stayed in the Egyptian capital for several weeks, during which time was one of the first Westerners to set foot in a mosque and to sketch the interior.
One of the conditions attached to this rare privilege was that he would not use paintbrushes

made with hog or boar bristles. In Cairo, Roberts made the acquaintance of Hanafee Ismail Effendi, a young Egyptian who converted to Christianity, who spoke fluent English, and who accompanied Roberts for the rest of his adventure. During that same period of time, he also met two English travellers, John Pell and John Kinnear. (Kinnear wrote an account of the journey, entitled "Cairo, Petra, and Idumea.")
In February 1839, they decided to venture across the desert as far as the Sinai, and then to visit the legendary Petra, and lastly, Palestine. Roberts split off from Kinnear at Gaza and headed for Jerusalem, arriving there at Easter. After touring the Jordan Valley and all of the major places in that area, he

In the years subsequent to the publication of "The Holy Land," David Roberts enjoyed a growing success with the public as well as great critical acclaim. Fascinated by biblical subjects and by the remarkable views of archeological sites

with an "exotic" flavor, such as Petra and Baalbec, a number of private clients commissioned him to do paintings based on the lithographs. Among the most illustrious of his private clients were Queen Victoria, the Countess of Warwick, and many other members of the British aristocracy and upper class.

continued northwards, skirting the Sea of Galilee and the major cities along the Lebanese coast. At Baalbec, he contracted an insistent fever, which prevented him from travelling on to Palmyra.

He was forced to head for Beirut, where he took ship for England on the 13th of May 1839. After returning to his homeland after an absence of eleven months, he submitted the fruit of his travels and labors to a great many publishers until he met Francis Graham Moon, who expressed the kind and degree of interest that Roberts was seeking. Moon offered Roberts three thousand pounds sterling for the rights to publish the work, and for his supervision of the etching of the printing plates. The lithographs that made up the three volumes of "The Holy Land, Syria, Idumea, Egypt, Nubia," which were published between 1842 and 1849, were executed by the thirty-four-year-old artist of Belgian origin, Louis Haghe. Haghe worked from the sketches and observations of Roberts himself. Their collaboration was particularly fruitful, and led to great things later on.

The technique that the young plate maker employed was particularly laborious; he executed each print in two colors and then completed the coloring by hand. For Roberts, the advantages that accrued from the publication of this book were chiefly in terms of glory and

renown since the compensation of three thousand pounds was quite small when compared to the immense amount of work and suffering that he underwent during his travels. Just two years after returning from his journey, Roberts was made a full member of the Royal Academy.

In the two decades that followed, the artist made numerous trips to various European countries, taking inspiration for a number of paintings and etchings that were shown with great success in the leading galleries of London and abroad. During his long career, Roberts received high honors and awards. Among the most prestigious of these came at the International Exposition of Paris in 1855. Five years later, he began work on a series of oil paintings whose common theme was the Thames River. Many of his later works were painted upon commission or sold as soon as they were completed; clear indicators of economic success. Surrounded by affectionate friends and respectful art critics, David Roberts died of a heart attack at the age of sixty-eight on the 25th of November 1864 and was buried in the cemetery of Norwood.

The ink sketches shown here (depicting Tyre, the Church of the Nativity in Bethlehem, Sidon, Jerusalem seen from the Mount of Olives, and Baalbec) accompanied a short note which indicated specific features, size, and price of every painting - a sort of "technical file" presented by the artist before completing the painting. These sketches are particularly interesting because they allow us to guess at what the preparatory drawings - sketched on the spot by Roberts during his journey through the Holy Land - must have looked like.

Page 22-23
View of Jerusalem from the Mount of Olives.

Page 24-25
View of the convent of St.Saba.

FROM SUEZ TO JERUSALEM

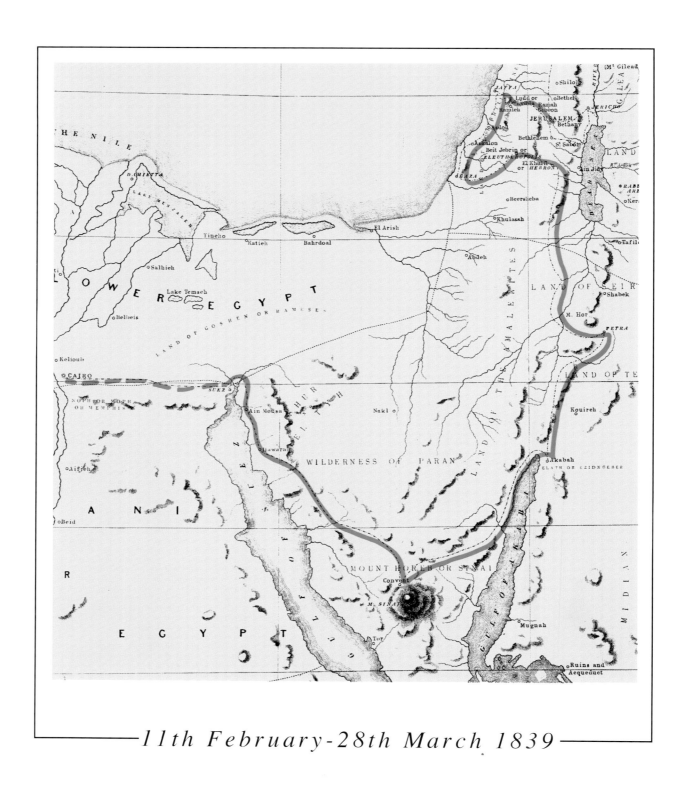

11th February-28th March 1839

David Roberts. R.A

HOLY LAND,

Syria, Idumea, Arabia, Egypt & Nubia.

FROM DRAWINGS MADE ON THE SPOT BY

David Roberts, R.A.

WITH HISTORICAL DESCRIPTIONS BY

THE REV.ᴰ GEORGE CROLY, L.L.D.

LITHOGRAPHED BY

LOUIS HAGHE.

VOL. 3.

LONDON, F. G. MOON, 20 THREADNEEDLE STREET,
PUBLISHER IN ORDINARY TO HER MAJESTY.
MDCCCXLIV.

ARRIVING IN SUEZ

Plate 1

10th February 1839

SUEZ. Feb. 11th 1839

Having left London on the 31st of August 1838, and having touched at ports in France, Italy, Malta, and the Greek islands, David Roberts reached Alexandria on the 24th of September. From here, Roberts set off along the Nile Valley; during that trip he sketched all of the principal monuments of the pharaohs. Returning to Cairo on the 21st of December, during the first days of the year Roberts decided to continue on to Syria, and to visit Jerusalem and the Holy Land. By the 21st of January, he had arranged for a number of camels and the appropriate equipment. On the same day, however, he received word of a serious outbreak of the plague in Judea, and that there was a strict "cordon sanitaire" around Jerusalem. To his great disappointment, Roberts decided to wait out events, and in the meanwhile he continued preparations for this new adventure. A week later, he finally learned that the time seemed ripe. On the 29th of January, he received from Colonel Campbell - the English general consul at Cairo - two letters of presentation to the consuls of Jerusalem and Damascus, and a safe-conduct signed by the pasha in person, so that anywhere he might need it he would immediately be supplied with an armed escort. In the meantime, Roberts had in part modified his plans, agreeing to join forces with two other English travellers, John Pell and John Kinnear. The new plan was to reach Palestine by following the route believed used by Moses, from Suez to Aqaba through the Sinai, and then following the valley of El Ghor all the way to Petra, and thence on to Hebron. The three Europeans decided to wear local garb, so much more practical in the brutal heat of the desert. Roberts, who intended to pay visits to a number of mosques, was also obliged to shorten his thick sideburns. The caravan was formed of twenty-one camels and escorted by nearly the same number of armed Beduins. The baggage included a number of tents, blankets, and weapons, along with adequate quantities of munitions and foodstuffs. The group left Cairo on 7th of February and was within sight of Suez and the Red Sea three days later, after following for a considerable distance a track marked only by the fossilized carcasses of camel after camel. On every hand was a featureless sun-beaten desert without a hint of tree or shrub in any direction. The city of Suez lay along the sea, and walls protected the side that was exposed to the interior.

On the opposite side of the Gulf and in sharp contrast with the motionless surface of the great body of water, stood the mountains of Sinai, reflecting the rays of the setting sun in a red fireball.

From David Roberts's journal:

7th February - Left Cairo for Mount Sinai, and slept in the desert.
8th and 9th - On our way. Overtaken by a rain storm on the evening of the 9th, and before we could get our tents pitched everything was in a big mess.

Suez

Plate 2

10th February 1839

Quay at Suez. February 11th 1839.

Roberts described Suez as being fairly picturesque, and was particularly impressed by the unusual shape of the boats in the port. The city, which stands on the site of the ancient city of Kolsum, was already fairly important in bygone eras as the way station in passing from the Red Sea to the Mediterranean, but it had declined to little more than a unassuming village when the English, in a joint undertaking with the pasha of Egypt, established regular trade with their colonies in the Far East across this isthmus. Suez thus became the destination of steamers arriving from Bombay and even from China. In a very short time, it had attained great importance, and the construction of the canal only increased the importance of the port city. In reality, the first efforts to drive a canal across the isthmus date from the age of the Pharaohs, and the maritime link was routed through a branch of the Nile all the way to Cairo, and through a manmade canal from Cairo to Suez. The passage was operational under Trajan, as well, and for a brief period during Arab rule. An early plan for a direct canal was developed during the sixteenth century in Venice, which wanted to attract the South and East Asian trade to the Mediterranean, but difficulties of all sorts hindered the project. The project actually got underway only when Napoleon had his engineers begin to make studies and draw up plans.

This preliminary work was rudely interrupted by the thunder of war, and it was not until 1833 that work started again, under the aegis of Mohammed Ali Pasha. Although Mohammed Ali was in favor of the project in principle, he did little more than to equivocate. In November 1846, the "Societé d'Études du Canal du Suez," which worked under the direction of the Italian engineer Luigi Negrelli, proceeded by fits and starts until 1854. Years later, the "Universal Company of the Suez Canal" was set up, with the engineer Ferdinand de Lesseps as the director. Actual digging began in April 1859 and continued for ten years. The canal was finally inaugurated on the 17th of November 1869 in the presence of the empress of France, Eugénie; in celebration of the occasion, of course, Giuseppe Verdi composed "Aida."

From David Roberts's journal:

10th Sunday - Suez picturesque. Made a few sketches. Boats curious in form; sea limpid and pure.

David Roberts R.A

ARABS OF THE DESERT

Plate 3

11th -12th February 1839

*R*oberts began
his voyage toward the Holy
Land on the morning of the 11th
of February, after clearing up a
troublesome misunderstanding
with his Arab companions.
The Englishman had in fact
discovered that a considerable
portion of the grain that had
been included in the baggage
borne by the camels was not
meant, as he had assumed, for
their nourishment, but would
be given to the tribes they met
along the way for planting,
because the harvest of the
previous year had been
extremely scanty. A few hours'
ride out of Suez, the caravan
was caught by surprise in a
sandstorm so brutal that by
noon Roberts and his travelling
companions were forced to pitch
tents and take shelter.
In contrast, the following day
was beautiful. The track ran
along the coast, with an
imposing mountain range
rearing up in the distance.
This was the place where the
waters of the Red Sea
supposedly opened up to let
Moses and the people of Israel
through, crashing closed again
upon their persecutors. Their
trip proceeded without any major
surprises, and as the landscape
rolled past Roberts was able to
observe their surroundings in

perfect calm. Among the Arabs
who made up his entourage, the
most noteworthy individual
was certainly a certain Beshara,
a native of the tribe of Beni
Sa'id. Beshara was gifted with
an agile intelligence, and he
accompanied Roberts all the
way to Aqaba. His portrait was
of particular interest, chiefly
because it faithfully reproduces
the clothing that the guide wore.
Like all desert Arabs, he wore an
ample shirt or smock, gathered

at the waist with a leather belt,
and a heavy wool mantle over
that. His legs were bare, and he
wore simple sandals on his feet.
His turban denotes an elevated
rank, since the more ordinary
sort of headgear is made up of
a simple strip of rough cloth
fastened with a loop of twine
or twisted cloth. This simple but
eminently functional outfit
is completed by the ubiquitous
broad-bladed curved knife, and
a blunderbuss.

Arabs of the Tribe of the Benisaid. Feby 17th 1839!

THE WELLS OF MOSES

Plate 4

On the afternoon of the 12th of February, the caravan reached the so-called Wells of Moses, a group of freshwater springs barely marked by a few scraggly palm trees. Biblical tradition has it that this was where the people of Israel reached the shore after their miraculous passage through the Red Sea.

The pools vary in number from season to season, ranging from a minimum of seven to a maximum of fifteen. The level of the water and its flow also vary greatly. At times, the pools overflow and produce little rivulets, while at other times the water is little more than a dampness in the soil. Though eminently drinkable, the water has a brackish taste that is less than appetizing, and only the blast of desert heat can persuade one readily to drink. Not far from the oasis, a number of fragments and the remains of walls indicate that in antiquity a small village once stood here. Eyun Mousa is the name of the place in Arabic; this is the only source of fresh water for miles around and is also the only place in this section of the Gulf of Suez where any planting is done. That evening Roberts noted in his journal that, although the spectacle of Beduins gathering around the evening fire might be picturesque and romantic, his weariness after travelling twenty miles across the desert by camel prevented him from drawing anything at all.

Wells of Moses. Wilderness of Tyh. February 12th.

From David Roberts's journal:

12th - In two hours we reached the Wells of Moses, which are fifteen in number. They are surrounded by a few stunted palm-trees, and the waters are not sweet but bitter...

David Roberts. R.A.

12th February 1839

From David Roberts's journal:

*13th - Our route still near the shore of
the Red Sea - the desert mountains,
though barren, are picturesque in form.
14th - We leave the coast, and enter
amid the mountains, of which to-day I
made a coloured sketch.*

Approach to Mount Sinai   Wady Barak Feby 17th 1839

THE APPROACH TO MOUNT SINAI

Page 5

13th–14th February 1839

The travellers broke camp at sunrise and the caravan set out once again along the track that ran along the coast of the Gulf of Suez amidst a landscape that was totally arid, but which had its own strange allure. The 13th passed without any noteworthy events and by four in the afternoon the tents had been pitched not far from a source of fresh water, Wadi Howara. Again, the next day, nothing occurred to interrupt the tranquil monotony of the voyage:

a cup of coffee upon rising, two hours of travel, and the customary halt to pray in the direction of Mecca, which the Arab entourage never forewent. Lunch meant finishing off the remains of the previous evening's meal and a few gulps of water from the waterskins. With some surprise, Roberts noticed that he ate these frugal meals with an

enjoyment he had not experienced since childhood. At sunset, the tents were set up in the oasis of Marah, where the fresh water was as welcome as a benediction amidst the desert blast. Upon the horizon, the travellers could already make out the outlying slopes of Mount Sinai—an improbable and solemn setting, where nature is the only lord, and, at the same time, the only witness, unchanged over the millennia to the passage of time. For time out of mind, despite all of the controversy fueled by historians and archaeologists, the Sinai has been associated with the Exodus, with the wanderings of the House of Israel, and with the Tablets that the Lord handed down to Moses: "And they took their journey from Elim, and all the congregation of the children of Israel came unto the wilderness of Sin, which is between Elim and Sinai, on the fifteenth day of the second month after their departing out of the land of Egypt." (Exodus, 16:1) Nonetheless, the Sinai has been more than simply the setting of biblical stories; it has been the backdrop for one of the most important events in human history—the development of the acceptance of the laws of a single God, although this was a people that grew and learned amidst a polytheistic society.

THE TEMPLE ON GEBEL GARABE

Plate 6

15th–16th February 1839

The 15th of February proved to be one long, grueling march of fifteen hours through the savage desolation of the Sinai. The solitude of the place was such that, although they had been on the move for five days, in all that time Roberts and his fellow travellers had encountered only two wayfarers, both heading for Egypt.

The track led on and on, driving ever deeper into the interior. The following morning before starting up the mountain called Gebel Garabe, the Arab guides sent ahead the camels with the tents, as from that point

twisting upwards to the peak of the rough hill. Here Roberts had the good fortune to stumble upon an ancient Egyptian temple, still exceedingly well preserved. The walls were covered with numerous hieroglyphics, royal cartouches, and symbolic figurations. Amidst the ruins stood about fifteen large stelae, and dozens more lay broken and scattered. These artifacts must have performed a votive function since the entire complex seems to have been a place of pilgrimage and may have been dedicated to Hathor. This supposition would seem to

forward they would only be a burden and no longer a help. For the first stretch, the path followed the bed of a wadi that had recently dried up, the sides of which were softened by a remarkable burst of desert blooms. Then the path led on through rock formations with the most unexpected shapes and curious colors; it then led

be supported by a number of capitals bearing the effigy of the good goddess, mistress of beauty and music. One of them can be seen clearly in the illustration, in the foreground. On the architrave, on the other hand, we can see the winged sun disc, symbol of the god Horus, exceedingly common in Egyptian temples.

Temple on Gebel Garabe, called Sarabit el Khadim. Feb 9

From David Roberts's journal:

*15th - Made three sketches, and
travelled fifteen hours through the
wilderness of Sinai, where the
Israelites were condemned to wander
for forty years...
16th - After much fatiguing climbing,
we reached the summit of the
mountain; and, to my amazement,
instead of a few stones, we found an
Egyptian temple in excellent
preservation...
I made a sketch of this, and felt very
much pleased at our discovery.*

THE ENCAMPMENT
AT THE FOOT OF MOUNT SERBAL

Plate 7

17th February 1839

Mount Sinai appeared almost suddenly in all of its majesty on the morning of the 17th of February; the path continued to become steeper and more hazardous. That evening, Roberts and his fellow travellers halted not far from an Arab camp, the first that they had encountered thus far in their journey. All around the camp, sheep and goats grazed unfettered. The new arrivals were greeted in a friendly way by the tribe of Aulad Sa'id, which extended its rule over the surrounding region. The men of the tribe boasted the title of Defenders of the Monastery of St. Catherine, and had done so for centuries. A baby goat was slaughtered in honor of the new guests, and soon the servants of the English artist were intent on roasting the goat over a brightly burning campfire.
The entire camp - in the midst of which the brightly colored tents of the expedition seemed quite garish in comparison with the austere shelters of the Beduins - was steeped in an immense quiet, even during a great variety of activities: a number of women were engaged in milling grain, other women baked bread, and crowds of youngsters were rounding up the livestock to be led to the pens. Overhead, the moon moved slowly across the sky. The tribe of Aulad Sa'id had taken up residence at the foot of Mount Serbal, an imposing massif of red granite, entirely bare of vegetation; many scholars have identified this as the Mountain of the Laws mentioned in the Bible. The fact that this is the first sizable mountain to be seen when arriving from the Gulf of Suez, the isolated location of the mountain, and its distinctly threatening appearance all combine to suggest that this peak, and not Gebel Mousa, may have been the peak upon which Moses received the Tablets of the Ten Commandments from God. The debate is still quite alive, and is probably destined to remain so forever. Nor could it be otherwise.

From David Roberts's journal:

17th - Mount Sinai burst upon our sight in all its splendour; and here we met, for the first time, with an Arab encampment, surrounded by flocks of sheep and goats.

THE ASCENT OF THE LOWER RANGE OF SINAI

Plate 8

18th February 1839

The caravan left the Arab camp around noon, heading for the Convent of St. Catherine; gradually, as the hours passed, the path became increasingly difficult, and the group of travellers were overwhelmed by fatigue.
The trail itself, long ago a remarkable piece of engineering, but now damaged extensively by landslides and collapses, wound up steeply along the sheer crumbling walls of a dark and savage gorge.
The spectacular view of the mountain peaks shimmering in the last light of sunset, in unsettling contrast with the darkness in which the deep belows lay swathed, indicated that night was falling quickly, and darkness was upon them long before they had sighted the monastery.
The track was broken and perilous, and often blocked by rubble that had tumbled from the high surrounding walls. For the group of travellers, dazed by fatigue, picking their way through that succession of rocky detritus was rapidly becoming a hazardous undertaking; finally the walls of the Convent of St. Catherine hove into sight not far away. In a short time, the caravan had succeeded in attracting the attention of the monks, who inquired as to the identity of the English traveller and his entourage.

Ascent of the lower range of Sinai.

The monks lit torches to illuminate the path and lowered a stout rope from a cabin that stood at a considerable height There was, in fact, no other way into the monastery, and so the various members of the expedition were hoisted up to the monastery by brute force, and they all had bruises to show for it. After being led through a maze of corridors and passageways, Roberts was welcomed with solemn courtesy by the abbot himself, who honored the customs of hospitality by offering the entire entourage rice soup and dates. A short while later, the artist was fast asleep in a comfortable bed.

From David Roberts's journal:

18th - Supper of rice and dried dates was set before us, and never did a poor pilgrim sleep more soundly than I did under the hospitable roof of the monks of Saint Catherine, Mount Sinai.

THE MONASTERY OF ST. CATHERINE

Plate 9

19th February 1839

We find the earliest information about the Monastery of St. Catherine in the chronicles of the patriarch of Alexandria, Eutychios, who lived in the ninth century. It is narrated here that Queen Helena, the mother of Emperor Constantine, during her pilgrimage to the holy places described in the Bible, came to the Sinai, and was able to find the exact place where the Burning Bush had appeared to Moses. The queen ordered a small chapel to be built, had it dedicated to the Virgin, and in a short while a monastic community gathered around the chapel.

In the years that followed, the convent increased in wealth, with ever more numerous ecclesiastical donations. As a result, the monastery increasingly fell prey to the incursions of desert pirates. In A.D. 530, Emperor Justinian ordered the construction of a great basilica, which later became the Church of the Transfiguration. In order to protect the monks from further attacks, he ordered that a veritable fortress be built around the complex. Following the Arab conquest of Egypt in A.D. 640, the convent became the last enclave of Christianity in the burgeoning Muslim world, ensured by the safe conduct issued to monks by the Prophet Mohammed himself. The monks still exhibit what they say is a copy of the very document Mohammed drew up. In A.D. 726, the iconoclast Emperor Leo III ordered the destruction of all sacred images, but the convent of St. Catherine, protected by its absolute isolation, was alone in conserving intact the enormous artistic patrimony. The tiny Christian diocese, still today the world's smallest, passed intact through the bloodiest years of the Crusades and over the ensuing centuries remained an oasis of peace and traquillity, periodically receiving the visit of one or another illustrious personality attracted by the allure of biblical places and the holy nature of the Church. Following Napoleon's expedition to Egypt, the Convent of St. Catherine was described widely in Europe, the beginning of a widening fame that has come down to the present day.

From David Roberts's journal:

19th - The convent is a large square enclosure, the walls and flanking towers built of hewn granite. Inside, it looks like a small town, for beside the apartments and store-houses there is a chapel and a mosque...

Convent of St. Catherine with Mount Horeb. Feby. 18th 1839.

David Roberts, R.A.

THE ASCENT TO THE SUMMIT OF SINAI

Plate 10

From David Roberts's journal:

20th February 1839

20th - To-day we ascended to the summit of Sinai, which took us two hours... The view from the top is the most sublime that can be imagined.

The mountainous massif that occupies the southern area of the Sinai peninsula, generally referred to as Mount Sinai, is in reality made up of four main peaks, all of them standing taller than six thousand five hundred feet above sea level; there are also a number of smaller peaks. It is impossible to establish which of these peaks is the one referred to in the Bible, where God gave the Tablets of the Law to Moses, but tradition tells us that the mountain in question is the Gebel Mousa, the peak that towers above the Convent of St. Catherine. Further obstacles to a straightforward interpretation derive from the fact that, in the Old Testament, Sinai - which is to say, the "mountain of God" - was often referred to as Horeb. Both names - Horeb and Sinai - are cited as the location of the vision of the Burning Bush, the Alliance, and the handing down of the Ten Commandments. This dual set of names has given rise to a set of differing interpretations, the most widely accepted among them being that Horeb was the name for the massif as a whole, and that Sinai was the name for the individual mountain that Moses climbed. Roberts must certainly have been persuaded by the last-mentioned hypothesis, as we can see from the notes that he made at the foot of his drawings. The day after he first reached the Convent of St. Catherine, the

artist decided to climb the mountain that was considered sacred to the three great monotheistic religions of the world. The climb took only a couple of hours. This was no mere outing, and the climb seems all the more daunting to a modern tourist if we consider that the path, which is extremely steep at points and quite precarious, was crumbling and exposed to avalanches in a number of points. The so-called "Stairway of Moses," shown here, covers the most difficult portion of the climb, and consists

of more than three hundred steps carved out of granite. Legend narrates that a single monk did the enormous labor involved, in order to keep a vow he had made. The stairway leads to the "Gate of Confessions," an arch where pilgrims made confession to one of the monks of the convent. Only after absolution could the faithful continue, reaching the "Gate of the Faithful," where they would remove their shoes and, barefoot before God just as Moses had been, finally climb to the summit.

Ascent to the Summit of Sinai. Feb.y 20th 1839

David Roberts R.A.

THE CHAPEL
OF ELIJAH

Plate 11

20th February 1839

*A*fter passing through the Gate of Confessions, the path rises over a little saddle or basin atop the ridge that separates the valley of St. Catherine from the parallel valley of El Leja. The peak of Gebel Mousa can at last be seen a short distance away, while further off rises the huge bulk of Gebel Katrina. From this point, the view penetrates freely all the way to the monastery below and to the nearby plain of El Rahah, over the expanses of peaks of the Sinai, and across the bone-dry wadis sunken in the bottom of the valleys. In the middle of the hill there grows a solitary cypress tree, not far from a fairly deep well and a boulder covered with inscriptions, the relic of an Islamic pilgrimage. Here, where the last stretch of the trail begins, stands a low construction known as the Chapel of Elijah, built upon the spot where the prophet supposedly sought refuge from the persecution of the Queen Jezebel, the idolatrous wife of Ahab, a follower of the god Ba'al and an enemy to Israel. Inside the small building, an altar marks the entrance to the cavern where Elijah supposedly lived until God appeared before him, comforting him and suggesting that he travel to Syria where he could continue his prophetic mission.

Chapel of Elijah on Mount Horeb. Feby 20th 1839

The Summit of Mount Sinai

Plate 12

The summit of Gebel Mousa, a massif formed predominantly of porphyry and of a distinctly colored red granite, is some 6,993 feet above sea level. Here, in the sixth century A.D., Emperor Justinian built a small chapel - destroyed and rebuilt any number of times - upon the spot in which Moses supposedly received the Ten Commandments from God. In a singular counterpoint with the Christian structure, a mosque - similarly small in size - marks the point from which, according to the lore of the Sinai Beduin, the holy prophet Nabi Saleh was elevated to Heaven. The mountain is sacred to Islam because Mohammed made a halt there during his night-long journey from Mecca to Mount Ararat. As a relic of this remarkable event, a pawprint of the Prophet's flying camel, Burack, is impressed in the living rock. Roberts, who had heard of this legend, wished to see the magical footprint with his own eyes. He had to agree that the impression looked exactly like a camel's pawprint, through some freak of nature. At the time of Roberts's visit, both the chapel and the mosque were in a state of sad disrepair, but during the 1930s, extensive repair work was done. Today, most pilgrims and tourists prefer to spend the night high on the summit, until the light of dawn illuminates all the surrounding peaks and inches its way out to the Gulf of Aqaba.

From David Roberts's journal:

20th - Near the top are two small chapels. One covers the cave where Elijah passed the night...
On the summit are other two - one where Moses received the tables of the law, the other belongs to the Mahometans, and under it is pointed out the foot-mark of the camel that carried the prophet...

20th February 1839

The Convent of St Catherine Mount Sinai, looking towards the Ruins of the Encampment. Feby 21st 1839.

THE MONASTERY OF ST. CATHERINE AND THE PLAIN OF THE ENCAMPMENT

Plate 13

21st February 1839

Downhill from the convent, along the wadi, there spreads a broad plain where biblical tradition holds that the people of Israel set up camp while waiting for Moses to descend from Mount Sinai. The Bible states, as a matter of fact, that "So Moses went down unto the people and spake unto them. And God spake all these words, saying, 'I am the Lord thy God, which have brought thee out of the Land of Egypt, out of the house of bondage. Thou shalt have no others gods before me.'" (Exodus, 19, 25; 20, 1:3.) Although it is extremely difficult to determine whether the story as told in the Bible corresponds to actual history, a series of careful scientific investigations has made it possible to cast new light on the daunting exodus of the Jews in the desert, a forty-year continual search for wells or a luxuriant oasis.

It is impossible to determine how many Jews left Egypt during the reign of Rameses II, but it is certainly unlikely that they were three million as the Bible states in Exodus. It is much more realistic to believe, as most scholars now do, that there were thirty thousand individuals,

who in all likelihood did not pass by the base of Gebel Mousa at all, but rather much farther north, where the oases are far more common. In any case, whatever the route that was followed by Moses and his people, these sites have always emanated an attraction that cannot be explained by reason alone. Roberts himself remained greatly impressed by the Sinai, and in particular by the Monastery of St. Catherine, which he sketched from a number of different angles. In this plate, where it is possible to see among other things the two tents used by the expedition, we can clearly see the minaret of the mosque that stands alongside the Church of the Transfiguration. In fact, inside the walls, a small Muslim community coexists in perfect harmony with the Christians—this unusual cohabitation is a result of the fact that the mountain is also greatly venerated in Islam. The need to protect the pilgrims of both religions helped to contribute to the preservation of the convent far more than the document signed by Mohammed, who is also believed to have founded the mosque.

The walls of the Monastery of St. Catherine

Plate 14

21st February 1839

Nestled at an altitude over five thousand feet above sea level at the end of a narrow valley, the Monastery of St. Catherine is made even more noteworthy by the setting of spectacular mountains that stand majestically circling it. In this illustration, the complex is portrayed in all the powerful splendor of its fortifications.
The appearance of the structure is believed to have changed very little since the Crusades.
The stout enclosing wall made of red-granite blocks girds an area that is roughly rectangular in shape, two hundred seventy-eight feet by two hundred forty feet.
The height of the walls ranges from forty to fifty feet; they attain a width of five and a half feet at the base. Numerous Maltese crosses are cut into the wall along its entire perimeter, with some of them dating from the reign of Justinian.
The eastern corner is protected by the Kleber Tower, while a number of other towers with square or circular plans soften the severity of the construction. Upon the northwest wall, at a height of about thirty feet off the ground, one can still clearly see the jutting cabin depicted by the English artist. Inside the cabin was a winch, which originally allowed visitors to enter the convent, as well as permitted supplies and other materials to be brought in. The original gate, which opened just slightly to the right in the walls, had in fact already been walled up since the Middle Ages so as to leave absolutely no openings in the walls at ground level. Modern-day visitors can enter the monastery through a narrow cranny, cut in the twentieth century and located beneath the trap door of the winch; a number of wells provide the convent's water supply.
The most important of these wells stands just to the right of the entrance on the inside and is known as Bir Mousa, or the Well of Moses. Tradition has it that it was here that Moses met the daughters of Jethro. The eldest among them, Zipporah, eventually became his wife. On the interior, the Monastery of St. Catherine seems almost like a medieval village made up of tiny courtyards, stairways, catwalks, vaulted galleries, and narrow corridors. The constructions are built one jutting up against the other, as if they had sprung up spontaneously with no particular order or intent in a remarkable mixture of varied styles and proportions.

THE CHURCH OF THE TRANSFIGURATION

Plate 15

21st February 1839

The saint to whom this monastery is consecrated was born in Alexandria in A.D. 294 with the name of Dorothea. She was born into a rich and aristocratic family. Extremely learned and well versed in philosophy, she became a Christian and was baptized Catherine. She confounded a great many wise men in a public debate in the presence of Emperor Maximinus Daia. She miraculously escaped death on the wheel, but was then martyred through decaptitation. She was buried in Alexandria, and five full centuries elapsed before a monk of the Sinai had a vision of the body of the saint, transported by angels to the peak of a nearby mountain, where the body remained, sweet-smelling and intact. In time, the monks decided to transport the saint's body to the nearby monastery, which from that moment forward took the name of the saint, as did the mountain, still known as Gebel Katrina. The saint's left hand and her skull, girt by a crown made of gold, studded with precious stones, were sealed up in exquisite silver coffers and placed in a sarcophagus next to the altar of the Church of the Transfiguration. This is one of the most ancient Christian basilicas to survive intact, as it originally appeared. The interior, one hundred thirty-one feet in length, is split up into three naves, punctuated by twelve monolithic granite columns which represent the months of the year. Each column is adorned with a massive carved capital, different from the other eleven, and bears an icon of the saint who is venerated during the corresponding month. The central nave terminates in an apse whose basin is covered with an exquisite mosaic dating from the sixth century, depicting the transfiguration of Christ; each of the side naves terminates in a chapel. Hanging from the eighteenth-century wooden ceiling, decorated with gold stars on a green background, are about fifty lamps made of gold-plated silver. In line with Greek Orthodox tradition, the altar is hidden from the sight of the faithful by the iconostasis, an exquisitely decorated partition. The iconostasis is formed of four wooden panels, with carvings and gold-leaf decoration, with icons of Christ, the Virgin Mary, Saint Catherine, and St. John the Baptist. High above the iconostasis stands an imposing Christ on the Cross. Both this Christ and the rest of the iconostasis were painted by Jeremiah of Crete, during the seventeenth century, and donated to the monastery by the Patriarch of Crete. Roberts was able to sketch the interior of the church through the kind intervention of the abbot; this same abbot, however, was reluctant to allow Roberts to sketch the chapel of the Burning Bush.

Chapel of The Convent of St. Catherine on Mount

THE MONKS OF THE MONASTERY OF ST. CATHERINE

Plate 16

21 février 1839

*E*ven now, the Monastery of St. Catherine is under the administration of the Greek-Orthodox Church. Most of the monks that live there are Greek Orthodox, and they practice the cult of St. Basil the Great, the bishop of Caesarea, who lived from A.D. 329 to 379. It is customary for the abbot of the monastery to be chosen by a majority vote, by a council formed of four archimandrites, then to be consecrated by the Patriarch of Jerusalem - one of six ecumenical Greek-Orthodox patriarchs (the other five are the Patriarchs of Rome, Moscow, Istanbul, Alexandria, and Antioch). In this illustration, which shows the courtyard of the monastery, Roberts devotes special attention to the clothing of the monks. The abbot, the archbishop of the Sinai, can be easily picked out from the crowd, as he is wearing a long black mantle, different from that of his brother monks. The garb worn by the entire community, in fact, was cut from a cloth made of camelhair and goathair, very similar to the clothing worn by Beduins; this cloth was made in the monastery. The monks, who never numbered more than twenty, saw to all their needs, and produced all the things that could be needed in that tiny universe. As the need arose, each monk became a carpenter, a woodsman, a tailor, a cobbler, a baker, and a chef. Most monks spent from three to five years at the Convent of St. Catherine, but some of the monks spent their entire lives there. The rules called for them to attend mass twice a day and never to eat meat. Roberts spent a great deal of time talking to the superior, an extremely learned and courteous individual, who had travelled extensively throughout Europe and to England; he had only the most pleasant memories of his travels.

THE ROCK OF MOSES

Plate 17

22nd February 1839

On the 22nd of February, Roberts bade farewell to the hospitable monks of the Monastery of St. Catherine, setting off again in the direction of Aqaba, where he expected to arrive within twenty-four hours. That same morning, quite early, the superior had arranged for the caravan to be sent on ahead, along with all the baggage, and by sunset, the English artist - who had stopped along the way to make some sketches - found camp already set up in a wadi to the west of the monastery. After crossing the mountain that separates the valley of St. Catherine from the valley of El-Leja, where the abandoned convent of El-Arbain is located, the artist stumbled upon the Rock of Moses, an enormous boulder that is venerated as the rock mentioned in the Bible, when the people of Israel were left without water, and began to complain. When this happened, Moses supplicated the Lord, who ordered him to take the rod with which he had caused the Red Sea to open, and told him "Behold, I will stand before thee there upon the rock in Horeb; and thou shalt smite the rock, and there shall come water out of it, that the people may drink." (Exodus, 17:6). Roberts believed that the boulder must have tumbled down from the side of the mountain in the distant past, and noted that on the surface of

the rock there were a dozen or so fairly regular channels. Careful observation led him to decide that this was not the work of human beings. Rather, he felt, when the boulder had been part of some cavity or cavern deep in the mountain, worn away by streams of water. More likely, however, the unusual shape of the Rock of Moses was the result of the continuous action of desert winds, which blow constantly here.

From David Roberts's journal:

22nd - Made a drawing of the Rock of Moses, said to be that from which the water gushed forth to the thirsty multitude. Took leave of our friends the monks of St. Catherine's, of whose kindness it is impossible to speak too highly...

Moses. Wady el Sheykh, Mount Horeb. Feb'y 22d 1839.

David Roberts R.

THE ISLE OF GRAIA,
GULF OF AQABA

Plate 18

23rd -27th February 1839

With a lively eye for details, Roberts mentioned in his journal that the 23rd of February began with a hike of a couple of hours' duration, followed by a halt to eat something: bread baked by the monks of St. Catherine, cold meat, butter from Cairo, dates, olives, and water diluted with a bit of brandy to soften its bitter taste. After smoking a pipeful of the finest Turkish tobacco, the caravan proceeded on its way through the hills of the Sinai; they pitched their tents at five in the afternoon, in the middle of a broad valley. The idea of reaching Aqaba quickly had evidently become impracticable, given the conditions of the track, and Roberts prepared himself cheerfully to continue riding for stretches of ten hours over the following days.

On the 24th of February, a Sunday, the expedition finally left the Sinai massif behind; now the landscape was reduced to a succession of low sandy hills dotted with bushes of wild thyme, with a fragrance that filled the heated air. In the afternoon, the track finally began to descend along a ravine that was savage and gloomy in appearance, and when they reached the end of it, suddenly, there were the coast and the crystal-clear waters of the Gulf of Aqaba. The following day, the scirocco wind that had sprung up in the south in the earliest hours of the morning had soon stiffened into a raging sandstorm, in the end forcing Roberts and his fellow travellers to pitch their tents in a sheltered bay. The heat was distinctly oppressive, and toward evening, the thermometer continued to hover at about 85 degrees F. The weather improved during the night, and by daylight the expedition was able to travel on with no further hindrance. On the evening of the 26th of February, finally, they made camp just before the Island of Graia, close to Aqaba. On the island, which was little more than a large rock, it was possible to make out the remains of a fortress or a city that - it was said - had flourished long before the Crusades. In effect, it is thought that the Citadel of Graia once formed part of the fortifications of nearby Eilat. Both Eilat and its neighbor, Aqaba, take their origins from Ezyon Geber, the Biblical port that was built by Solomon on the shores of the Red Sea. Occupied by Nabateans, Romans, Byzantines, and Arabs, it was finally destroyed by a Crusader army around 1116, during the siege of Eilat.

Isle of Graia Gulf of Akabah — Arabia Petraea

David Roberts R. A

THE FORTRESS OF AQABA

Plate 19

*T*he drinking water that the caravan had carried with it had long since run out when the caravan finally came to the walls of the fortress of Aqaba, at midday on the 27th of February. The garrison welcomed the unannounced visitors with great courtesy and offered them beds and blankets in the barracks room.

The English artist nonetheless preferred to pitch his tent outdoors and sleep there. After washing up and changing his clothing, he paid his respects to the local governor, an extremely genial and kind individual who offered the visiting foreigner some excellent coffee and tobacco.

After enquiring as to Roberts's route and destinations, he immediately ordered that a messenger be sent to the chief of the Alloueens. He said that without the authorization of the chief, the expedition absolutely could not proceed in the direction of Petra. The fortress, a massive structure with a square plan and a tower at each of the four corners, had been built around the middle of the sixteenth century by the Egyptian sultan el Ghoury, and served to protect pilgrims heading for Mecca, or returning from there to Egypt and to Syria. The strategic importance of the fort consisted largely of its proximity to a number of freshwater wells, the only ones for a great distance around, which represented a fundamental and vital supply resource for the caravans.

Although Roberts was unsuccessful in his efforts to find remains or inscriptions that dated back previous to the foundation of the fortress, he felt reasonably sure that this was the site of the ancient Aelana, the city of the Edomites, conquered by David. Near Aelana, Solomon founded Ezion Geber, which became one of the most important mercantile and commercial centers in the ancient world. While waiting for the chief of the Alloueens to reach Aqaba to begin negotiations, Roberts spent a couple of days bumming around the area and resting up for the tiring march to Petra.

From David Roberts's journal:

27th - We hurried on to the fortress of Akabah, where we arrived about 12 noon, our camels and Arab attendants apparently making a great impression on the inmates of the pigmy fortress... March 2nd - This morning the sheikh of the Alloueens arrived, when a grand palaver took place. After much beating about the bush, we came to terms, and he guaranteed our safe passage to Hebron, by the way of Wady Mousa or Petra, staying at the latter place as long as we chose...

27th February–1st March 1839

THE APPROACH TO PETRA

Plate 20

2nd-5th March 1839

The lively discussion between Roberts and the sheik of the tribe of the Alloueens, who had reached Aqaba during the morning of the 2nd of March, lasted for quite a while and ended on the following terms: If forty-five hundred piasters - equivalent to about forty-five pounds sterling at the exchange of the time - were paid, the caravan would be allowed to continue toward Hebron, crossing Wadi Mousa, and stopping at Petra for the amount of time Roberts would need to sketch the main monuments there. After striking this bargain, Roberts invited the sheik and the governor of Aqaba to dine in his tent, along with their lieutenants. Later Roberts bade farewell to the men of the tribe of Beni Sa'id who had accompanied him to that point, and began to prepare for his departure the next day. The new caravan, consisting of twenty-three beasts of burden, set off at dawn, and soon left behind the Gulf of Aqaba, striking out along what had once been the bed of the Jordan River thousands of years before. The plain was enveloped in a dense, suffocating fog, which made the desert that much more grim. The travellers moved along in silence until it was time to pitch tents; that same night the pale light of the full moon and the mysterious appearance of the mountains all around them cast Roberts into a strange state of mind, filling him with a yearning homesickness. The sheik's camp appeared on the horizon during the afternoon of the following day, and a few hours later the caravan was received with great joy. As a mark of hospitality to the three Westerners, a suckling goat was served, and they gladly accepted this kindness. After a peaceful night, the expedition set off once again at the first light of dawn, drawing closer to the outlying slopes of Mount Hor. At three in the afternoon, they set up camp beneath an ancient watchtower, set to guard the valley of El Ghor, one of the routes giving access to the city of Petra. The building, two stories high and absolutely free of adornment, stood in a remarkable location, at the peak of a rocky ridge jutting out over the level of the wadi. The tower must have once formed part of a series of watchposts or even a complex signalling system set up to guard the city. It should be noted that the date set on the plate, just as is the case elsewhere in the work of Roberts, is strangely inaccurate, and does not agree with what Roberts noted in his journal.

roach to PETRA – An Ancient Watchtower Commanding the Valley of El Ghor   Feb.y 5.th 1839

From David Roberts's journal:

4th - About 4 o'clock we arrived at the tents of the sheikh, where we were received with great kindness, and kissed on each cheek by every Arab present...
5th - Started early, as usual. About 12 o'clock we struck into a chain of mountains on our right, forming part of the range of Mount Hor. At 3 o'clock we pitched our tents at the entrance to Wady Mousa...

MOUNT HOR

Plate 21

Gebil Hor March 5th 1839

R.A

Made impatient by emotion, Roberts wished at all costs to climb to the peak of the hill that dominated the campground in order to take a first look at the mythical city of Petra, but his hopes were soon dashed by a further series of hills - completely unlooked for - which stood in the sight of the spot. The landscape, in any case, was spectacular, and the English artist felt wholly repaid for the effort involved in reaching the top of the hill. Beneath his feet were the ravines of El Ghor and Wadi Arabah, the rocks of Mt. Seir glittered in the splendid sunset, and in the distance, directly before him, towered the majestic bulk of Mt. Hor, at the foot of which the people of Israel pitched their tents after the flight from Egypt. It was here that the destiny of Aaron was fulfilled, when the Lord ordered Moses to lead him to the summit of the mountain. "And Moses stripped Aaron of his garments and put them upon Elea'zar his son; and Aaron died there on the top of the mount: and Moses and Elea'zar came down from the mount. And when all the congregation saw that Aaron was dead, they mourned for Aaron thirty days, even all the house of Israel" (Book of Numbers, 20, 28-29).

THE ENTRANCE TO PETRA

Plate 22

From David Roberts's journal:

6th - Petra. To-day we encamped in the centre of the remains of this extraordinary city, which is situated in the midst of mountains, surrounded by the desert, but abounding in every vegetable production...

6th March 1839

*A*t dawn on 6th of March, after the sheik tried in vain to persuade Roberts to leave his camels and baggage behind him in the camp and to continue on foot, the caravan set off once again and began to climb a steep trail that led along the edge of a precipice, amidst patches of oleander and laurel. After climbing a particularly difficult ridge, and as they were about to descend into the valley of Petra, Roberts and his Alloueen guides were stopped by a group of Arabs belonging to the tribe of Wadi Mousa, who commanded the city in the rock and all the surrounding region. Following a violent quarrel, their sheik informed the foreigners that there were ancient feuds between the two tribes and that the Alloueens had no right to enter Petra, nor to bring foreigners with them to Petra. Negotiations continued for a long time in extremely tense language, and in the end Roberts agreed to pay a tribute of three hundred piasters in exchange for permission to camp for five days in Petra without being disturbed. The time agreed upon was sufficient for the needs of the artist, but Roberts was forced to work during the entire time of his stay there. After passing by the barrier of the armed men, the caravan was able to descend to the floor of the valley, where they pitched their tents and watered their camels and then

led them to pasture.
The place where Petra stands is shaped like an amphitheater closed in by sheer cliffs, measuring roughly two-thirds of a mile from east to west and a third of a mile from north to south. The bed of a stream runs through the place and, with its tributaries, marks a low ridge upon which the proper city once stood. The cliffs that surround it, and which in certain points stand over nine hundred eighty

feet tall, were used as a medium in which to cut both tombs and habitations. Atop the surrounding peaks were located a number of places of worship and small forts that surveyed the roads leading into the town. The cavea of the theater, which can be seen in the foreground in the illustration, could hold as many as three thousand spectators and was entirely cut out of the side of the mountain.

Conference of Arabs at Petra

Plate 23

6th March 1839

*A*s soon as camp had been set up amidst the ruins of Petra, Roberts had an opportunity to witness an odd dispute amongst the very same Beduins who just a few hours before had so rudely blocked his way. One of the Arabs had been accused of stealing an ass, and in order to settle the matter, three sheiks of the tribe were asked to deliver their opinions. One of these sheiks, an elderly man held in great estimation by all, had the parties to the dispute sit upon the ground, arrayed in a circle, and began the council by reciting in the most solemn imaginable manner a part of the introductory chapter of the Koran, and a number of phrases that seemed to the ears of Roberts to be enunciations of fundamental laws. During the whole time he was speaking, the old man brandished a sword in his right hand, and the others listened carefully, occasionally nodding in silence. When the first sheik had set forth his view of things, he passed the sword to the next, who spoke in turn; this ceremony continued until all those who were present had spoken. During all this, no one had at any time dared to interrupt the speaker who had, as it were, the floor.

Once a decision had been handed down, the Arabs disappeared silently amongst the rocks. Although his curiosity was greatly aroused, Roberts was unable to find out what the verdict of that odd court had been, nor what the penalty inflicted might have been.

PETRA

Plate 24

6th March 1839

*L*ocated in southern Transjordan, Petra is mentioned several times in the Bible by the name of Sela, while the Arabs refer to it as Wadi Mousa, i.e. the Valley of Moses. Although the earliest habitations in the area date from the Iron Age, the city became important when the Nabateans occupied the region, during the period of Persian rule. Setting up their stronghold high atop one of the rocky spurs in the area, the Nabateans managed to hold out against the attempt by Antigonus I of Syria, in 312 B.C., to take the place by storm. Petra developed as a rock city at the intersection of three mountain gorges. Later it became a center offering haven and defense for the local nomadic populations.

The decision by the Nabateans to choose Petra as their capital was therefore based on considerations of security. Hidden as it was in the mountains, with a very few, easily guarded points of access, Petra constituted a secure safeguard for the wealth that the Nabateans had accumulated with their caravan trade.

The ease of communications with the Red Sea made it possible for the Nabateans to trade extensively with Arabia and with Mesopotamia, while the track through the Negev Desert to Gaza gave them access to the Mediterranean and to Syria.

The continuing development of major trade routes and the growing prosperity of the Nabateans themselves led to the growth of Petra, and to its eventual Hellenization.

In particular, during the first century A.D., the Nabatean kings embellished the town with splendid monuments, most of which were carved into the living rock. Roman occupation and the creation of the Arabian province slowed the development of Petra, but failed to halt it entirely.

In the third century A.D., however, with the transfer of the Nabatean capital to Bosra, and the growth of new caravan centers, such as Gerasa and Palmyra, in particular, the importance of Petra declined greatly, even though Emperor Hadrian bestowed upon the town the honor of the title of "metropolis."

For a number of centuries, the rock-cut city continued to be a major power, the see of a bishop, and, following the reorganization of the empire at the order of Diocletian, the capital of the province of Palaestina Taertia. After the Arab conquest, however, Petra declined greatly, though it was fortified and inhabited by the Crusaders. Following the thirteenth century, it was abandoned, and all knowledge of Petra was lost until the beginning of the nineteenth century.

El Khasnè

Plate 25

6th March 1839

Just as soon as camp had been been made, Roberts decided to go and see the Khasnè, certainly the best-known monument in Petra, as well as one of the wonders of the ancient world. In order to better understand the profound impact that the sudden appearance of this superb creation of human genius has upon the visitor, it should be noted that Petra is located in an extremely secure location, since the only easy access to the place is set to the east, and consists of a narrow stream bed enclosed by two cliff walls that are separated from each other in certain points by no more than twelve feet. This passage, now known as the Sik, is about two and a half miles in length. In ancient times, the water that once ran in the stream was channeled through a gallery carved into the rock some two hundred thirty feet in length, and its waters were partly conveyed in the city aqueduct. At a number of different points, caravansaries and spaces were set aside for the encampment of arriving caravans. About halfway up, at a point where the Sik suddenly changes direction, carved into the cliff, one can see the Khasnè, a funerary temple that has no · rival on earth. The contrast between the delicate pink facade of the building and the shadowy Sik is quite impressive. The symmetry of the facade is absolute, the proportions are exquisitely tasteful, and the degree of conservation is practically perfect. Roberts tended to believe that the Khasnè had been a mausoleum rather than a sanctuary, and yet, in connection with the age-old question of just what had been the real purpose of the similar structures lined up along the main valley, he expressed the opinion that they had been neither tombs nor temples, but built simply to titillate the refined esthetic tastes of the Nabateans, endowing the city with an openness of perspective that its remarkable natural location would otherwise have denied it. Excavations and careful studies have instead allowed us to determine that the rock-cut structures were put to a great number of uses and that a number of them were simply houses, often made of a large room with columns and niches on the sides and a raised triclinium in the center. A number of these residences are decorated with painted frescoes depicting grape vines and floral motifs

From David Roberts's journal:

6th - Our first stroll was to the Khasnè, and I cannot say whether I was most surprised at the building or its extraordinary position. It stands, as it were, in an immense niche in the rocks, and the fine colour of the stone, and perfect preservation of the minute details, give it the appearance of having been recently finished...

VIEW OF EL KHASNÈ, OR THE TREASURY

Plate 26

7th March 1839

*T*he facade of the Khasnè, one hundred thirty-one feet high and eighty-two feet long, is divided into two stories, the lower story consisting of a portico with pediment, with six Corinthian columns, over forty feet tall each. Between the two outer pairs of columns are two colossal equestrian groups executed in high relief. The design of the frieze consists of a series of pairs of gryphons facing each other, while the pediment, at the center of which stood an eagle with outspread wings, was completed by a scroll decoration. At the corners of the architrave, two lions served as acroteria.

The second story, of an airy elegance, is split into three pavilions. The central pavilion was a round tholos, practically a small-scale temple, with a conical roof surmounted by an urn. It is worth noting that this detail gave the building its name: In Arabic, El Khasnè means "treasury."

The Beduins believed that great wealth was concealed inside the urn and they regularly fired their rifles at it in order to shatter it, believing that a shower of riches would ensue. The tholos is flanked by two semi-pediments, each supported by four corner columns. In the niches stood reliefs representing female figures and four giant eagles served as acroteria. The interior of the building consists of a vestibule some forty-six feet wide and nineteen feet deep, and a stairway with eight steps leads to a central chamber. The chamber is a large cube, thirty-nine feet to a side, with three smaller rooms on each side. Two other smaller rooms lead off from the vestibule. It is this arrangement of interior rooms and the absence of any altar whatsoever, as well as the location of the building in the narrow gorge - which would certainly have hindered its functions as a temple - that leads us to suppose that the Khasnè was actually a monumental tomb, rather than a temple as had long been believed.

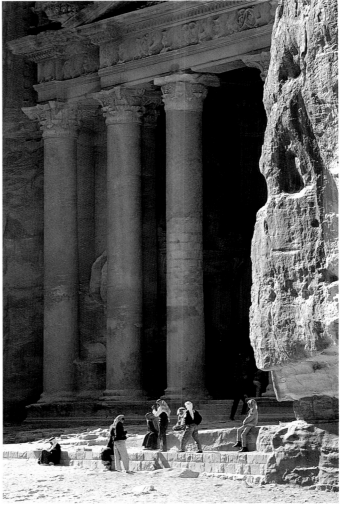

Temple called El Khasné Petra March 7th 1839

David Roberts R.A.

Louis Haghe 1849.

PETRA March 7th 1839.

THE EXCAVATED MANSIONS

Plate 27

7th March 1839

It was said that the Nabateans were the descendents of Nabath, the firstborn son of Ishmael. They did speak an Aramaic dialect, known as Mendaic, belonging to the northern branch of the Semitic languages. Originally, nomads from the Arabian peninsula, the Nabateans settled down and quickly organized themselves into a powerful centralized monarchy, and in a brief time prospered greatly.

The greatest point of expansion of the Nabatean kingdom came during Hellenic and Roman times, when the city of Petra flourished in a particularly spectacular manner.

The splendid capital of the Nabateans was, even in antiquity, the object of great amazement and surprise because of its unusual and spectacular appearance.

What is now the bed of the Wadi Mousa was then the main street of the town, beginning near a pool for the bath, alongside a nymphaeum; further on stood three marketplaces arranged on terraces one atop the other with shops arranged along the sides, a great Corinthian temple, baths, the Roman arch, and a several-storied gymnasium.

The rock cliff across from the theater contains a great many rock structures, all built with remarkable craftsmanship. The structure shown in the illustration is certainly one of the most interesting of them, both in terms of high quality of the workmanship and because of the setback of the facade with respect to the natural profile of the mountain face. There was certainly an unusual technical solution in the use of a double order of vaulted galleries to support the broad terrace between the two lateral colonnades cut into the living rock. The conscious attempt to attain a spectacular effect is hard to miss, and the result is made even more impressive by the warm tones of the stone.

From David Roberts's journal:

7th - I am more and more astonished and bewildered with this wonderful city, which must be five or six miles each way in extent; and every ravine has been inhabited, even to the tops of the mountains. The valley has been filled with temples, public buildings, triumphal arches, and bridges, all of which have been laid prostrate, with the exception of one arch, and one temple, and of this temple the portico has fallen. The style of the architecture varies from all I have ever seen and in many of its parts is a curious combination of the Egyptian with the Roman and Greek orders. The stream still flows through it as heretofore; the shrubs and wild-flowers flourish luxuriantly; every crevice of the rock is filled with them, and the air is perfumed with the most delicious fragrance.

El Deir

Plate 28

8th March 1839

On the morning of the 8th of March, Roberts started down a long ravine, accompanied by a small platoon of armed men. He was following an extremely rough trail, which soon turned into a steep stairway nearly a mile in length. After climbing nearly a thousand feet, the little group finally reached the astonishing rock-cut monument known as El Deir, which means the Monastery, one of the buildings in the ancient Nabatean capital that is less frequently visited, although it is certainly the most imposing. Cut entirely from living rock, the facade of the temple is one hundred and sixty feet in width and one hundred and twenty-eight feet in height; the decoration is very similar to that of the Khasnè, if only more elaborate. The lower floor is punctuated by eight columns that frame two arched niches, and a portal with a pediment in the center. Through the entrance, a double flight of steps leads to a square chamber. At the center of this chamber, the altar once stood, and is now almost entirely destroyed. Roberts observed a roughly painted cross upon the altar, a clear indicator that the pagan sanctuary had been used as a Christian church for a certain period. On the upper story, the facade, which is purely decorative in function, presents a central tholos, and the pediment, and two pillars at the corners, while a handsome Doric frieze crosses the entire facade. Facing this remarkable building, in a commanding position high on a natural base, stand the ruins of a second temple, preceded by a colonnade of which only the plinths survive. Roberts was intrigued by the incredible view that one enjoys from that rock balcony, projecting out over the valley of El Ghor. Indeed, Roberts became quite discouraged, and felt that he was not adequate to the challenge of depicting such marvelous creations.

8th - To-day we wound our way up a steep ravine, a broken staircase extending about a mile. We reached a bulding, rarely visited, called Deir, or Convent, which is hewn out of the face of the rock...
The view here is magnificent, embracing the valley of El Ghor, Mount Hor (the tomb of Aaron crowning the summit), and the whole defile, leading through rocks which make you giddy to look over; while the ancient city, in all its extent, is seen stretching along the valley...

THE EASTERNMOST POINT IN THE VALLEY

Plate 29

8th March 1839

*T*he first rock-cut monuments of Petra presented a smooth, extremely simple facade, surmounted by one or two rows of step pinnacles, at the base of which a door opened, at times framed by half-columns (this type of architecture can be seen in Plate 24). This sort of sepulchre, the oldest instances of which can be dated back to the end of the second century B.C., constituted a typically Nabatean adaptation of models that had become common in nearby Syria. During the two following centuries, more complex types of facades were developed. At the origin of this new development lay the adoption upon a broad scale of Hellenistic architectural motifs, such as the frieze, the architrave, and the pilaster strip. In the meanwhile, a special type of capital had been developed, which was known as the Nabatean capital, and an increasingly widespread use of structural elements with a purely ornamental purpose had spread. The extremely provincial nature of local art, which had developed in an area on the far boundaries of the civilized world, in open desert, nonetheless justified the persistence of local features in decoration that could be said to be completely obsolete, such as rosettes and animals used in a heraldic manner. In the second half of the first century A.D. a new type of facade finally made its appearance, enjoying its greatest degree of development in the following decades.

A noteworthy enrichment of an architecturally oriented range of figurative elements corresponded to an effort to develop the theatrically spectacular, which is so typical of Roman influence.

The cliff facades attained a colossal scale, with stacked orders of columns that served to emulate elevations of temples and theatrical "scenae."

During this period of great architectural production, the two tombs shown here in the illustration by Roberts were built, and still stand at the easternmost extremity of the valley: the so-called Tomb of the Palace, with four entrances with alternating arches and pediments and four orders of small columns and pillars on the upper order, is one; the other is the adjacent Corinthian Tomb, not unlike the Khasnè, but with a smaller, intermediate story between the pediment and the tholos.

THE RUINS OF A TRIUMPHAL ARCH

Plate 30

8th March 1839

Not far from the gymnasium, before which stood a great temple, the road passed under a triumphal arch characterized by three openings of considerable size. Although the structure had long since been reduced to a heap of rubble, the function it clearly served and the surviving bits of architecture that could still be deciphered indicated that this was a work dating back to Roman times. Numerous fragments of sculpture scattered all about showed that the arch had possessed a rather exuberant ornamentation. Amidst the ruins, among other things, there was a winged figure of remarkable workmanship that may well have had a place in the pediment. All through the area of what was once Petra, in fact, the presence of a great many decorative elements, which clearly reflected a Greco-Roman influence, leads us to think that after the Roman conquest of Petra in A.D. 106, master craftsmen who had come from the West were active in Petra. Nonetheless, the local style had characteristics of its own so distinct and recognizable that a clear identity arose without getting confused with the foreign styles. This illustration is dated the 8th of March, the third day of Roberts's stay in the Nabatean capital. That afternoon, while Roberts was away exploring and the servants were busy preparing dinner, a man succeeded in slipping into the camp and stealing a metal soup tureen, probably believing it to be silver. After vanishing among the rocks, the thief suddenly appeared atop a nearby peak and, brandishing his booty over his head, began to boast shamelessly of his prowess, and to promise new feats of thievery. The local tribes had a villainous reputation and their raids could easily end in tragedy for the unfortunate victims.

Petra, looking south

Plate 31

9th March 1839

The ruins of Petra were discovered by the Swiss Orientalist and traveller Johann Ludwig Burckhardt in 1812, and they certainly constitute one of the most singular and enchanting monumental complexes of the ancient world. There are two sets of reasons: first, the exceptional quality of the architectural creations themselves; and second, the odd and perhaps unique location of the city, clamped between volcanic hills, set deep in narrow gorges, enhanced by the remarkable color of the rock from which the buildings have been carved. This illustration clearly emphasizes the way in which the most significant surviving ruins line the main valley, perched on terraces at various levels; originally the terraces were linked one to the other by networks of stairways that must surely have been spectacular to see. As mentioned earlier, the stream bed must have been covered with a paved road, and the ruins that can be seen along each of the two banks indicate that this decuman of sorts was lined with a number of remarkable public buildings. On the northern side of the stream bed, in fact, the ruins of a very large temple can be observed, while on the opposite side, it is still possible to distinguish the outline of a monumental portico: not far off, where the main stream bed joins a creek of more modest dimensions, stand the remains of a broad terrace. At one side of this structure stood a small structure with a circular plan. Roberts was the first Westerner to receive official permission to camp at Petra, where he studied the monuments in some depth. He was also the first Westerner to bring back a thorough going graphic documentation of the place, while the first systematic archeological campaign was not carried out until much later, in the years from 1929 to 1935.

THE RAVINE, LEADING TO PETRA

Plate 32

9th March 1839

On the 9th of March, Roberts visited the main entry route to Petra, known as the Sik, a spectacular gorge about a mile in length, which runs right up to the temple of El Khasnè. Obscure, unsettling, and intriguing, the canyon is extremely narrow, perennially immersed in shadows, and clamped between cliff walls that rise from three hundred to six hundred feet high. At certain points the cliff walls almost seem to touch, blocking out any sky whatsoever. The rock appears to be shaped by the erosive action of the wind and by the erosion of a small stream, a stream that swells enormously, however, during the summer thunderstorms.

This unimpressive stream that now gurgles along in the open air, giving life to a tenacious vegetation, was once channeled along in an underground passage that was uncovered centuries ago. The illustration

shows an arch that once spanned the bottom of the canyon, connecting the two walls and reaching upwards to a considerable height; the lower section of the arch structure was cut out of the living rock and was decorated with two very deep niches, presumably meant to hold the simulacra of the patron deities of Petra. Although Roberts was unable to ascertain the original function of the striking piece of architecture, a number of fragments of a portal discovered on the canyon floor inspired the idea that this might have been a piece of defensive fortifications. Though Petra had long been uninhabited, Arab traders still made frequent use of the ancient track; in fact, while the artist sat sketching out this view, a caravan originating from Gaza went by on its way to Maan, along the Damascus road. The caravan was made up of about forty camels.

From David Roberts's journal:

9th - Explored the grand entrance to Petra, which may be about a mile in length, winding between the high rocks by which the Valley is enclosed, in many parts overhanging so as almost to meet each other... This was the grand entrance into Petra, and is still used by the Arabs.

David Roberts R.A.   Triumphal arch crossing the Ravine leading to
                                                              Petra.

THE ACROPOLIS
AND THE KUSR FARON

<u>Plate 33</u>

9th March 1839

*I*mmediately following the great theater, the gorge known as the Sik opens out into a broad and brightly illuminated valley, once packed with homes and temples, many of which have been unfortunately lost due to the violent flooding of the stream. During the time of Petra's greatest glory, the population must have ranged from thirty to forty thousand, most of whom were merchants and traders. At the center of the valley stands the hill now called El Habis, the site of the ancient Acropolis. From the slopes of this hill ran a wall that served to protect all of the main public buildings. The huge blocks of stone, which can be seen in the drawing, formed part of the triumphal arch; nearby a paved plaza once stood, though only a few scanty traces remain of it. At the extremity of the plaza closest to the Citadel stood an impressive building called Kusr Faron, which means the Castle of the Pharaoh. Although the complex stands for the most part in ruins, and we are uncertain as to its true function, its importance is noteworthy because we can draw some understanding from its overall appearance as to just what the appearance of the elevations of the buildings of ancient Petra must have been. Because the entire region is often subject to earthquakes, only the structures cut deep into the rock faces have remained much as they originally appeared, while virtually all of the other buildings have been destroyed. The facade of Kusr Faron presented a portico with four columns and with a single entrance leading to a fairly spacious hall within.

From this area, by climbing three stairways, one could enter as many different smaller rooms. The fact that the central hall should possess a sort of naos or "sancta sanctorum" surrounded by columns, leads us to believe that the so-called Castle of the Pharaoh was in fact a sanctuary. The facade, which measures about one hundred and five feet across, was also decorated with an elegant Doric frieze.

THE SEPULCHRAL MONUMENTS

Plate 34

9th March 1839

The rocky cliffs that surround the city served as raw material for the construction of both residences and tombs. And, as tombs go, the most remarkable and interesting monumental structures were carved out of solid rock along the great flank of the mountain, Gebel el Kubtha, to the west of the city proper. The earliest rock-cut tombs at Petra, dating from the third century B.C., or earlier, usually feature tall rectangular facades lined with lined battlements, clear indicators of Egyptian or Assyrian influence. Belonging to the Hellenistic and Roman era, on the other hand, a time that was so much wealthier in the creation of remarkable architecture, are the facades that we could almost describe as baroque - they rise several stories, they are distinguished by the free-form alternation of triangular and curvilinear pediments, and diverse architectural orders. These astounding elevations, minutely chiseled into the limestone, show a clear kinship with the fantastic architecture featured in the painting of the second Pompeian style. Just like in those celebrated frescoes, here the manner in which the upper story is conceived reveals an intention of endowing them with a certain added perspective with respect to the ground floor, by means of a meticulous interplay of slight optical corrections. On the interiors the tombs typically possess a number of rooms cut out of the rock: the typical plan is made up of a vestibule that gives access to the funerary chambers, smaller in size. In a number of cases, as Roberts himself noted, previously existing rock-cut habitations were converted into tombs. In the illustration on the left we can see a number of the most remarkable rock-cut tombs in the area. These are enormous monolithic cubes, which emerge from the slope of the mountain's face, as a result of a truly monumental effort in excavation. The tomb in the foreground caught the artist's attention because the plinths of the columns, the capitals, the architrave, and the cornices must all have been carved out of a particularly valuable material, either marble or bronze, and then set in the living rock. The material had long ago been torn away by some tomb robber, and by the time Roberts arrived, nothing was left but the notches which had held the ornamental finish. The rock-cut tomb in the background, still in an excellent state of preservation, is surmounted by four graceful pyramids, the only ones of their sort ever found at Petra. Roberts visited the necropolis on the 9th of March; the following day, the weather turned ugly and a steady rain fell. Nonetheless, the Englishman ventured forth to continue his exploration of the valley and its astounding ruins.

March 9th 1839

David Roberts. R. A.

From David Roberts's journal:

9th - The necropolis lies between the main entrance and the meadows; some of the tombs hewn out of the rock, though mutilated, are still magnificent. Several have porticoes and colonnades, and the columns of one I observed were Doric of the purest kind. They seem now to be used as pens for cattle.

THE TOMB OF AARON, SUMMIT OF MOUNT HOR

Plate 35

11th March 1839

On the morning of the 11th of March, the fifth day that Roberts spent at Petra, the camp was suddenly awakened by the shrill yells of desert bandits, who fled with their booty, a pair of pistols and a bag of cartridges. Considering what had happened, Roberts came to the suspicion that the attack had been arranged in advance with the local guides, who in fact seemed quite anxious to turn back at this point. At eight in the morning, the camels were saddled and, shortly thereafter, the caravan was climbing the mountains in a southeasterly direction. The sides of the mountains were dug out and the architectural forms quite resembled those that they had seen in the city. Not far from the peak stood a number of monuments whose significance was far from simple to interpret. At least, keeping Mount Hor on the right, the travellers began to climb back down toward the main valley, along a very steep track cut into the living rock like a rough stairway. Roberts deeply regretted being unable to climb to the Tomb of Aaron, but his shoes at this point were truly too worn for the task. It is therefore rather strange that this plate, dated precisely 11th March 1839, should depict the peak of Mount Hor and the sepulchre of the older brother of Moses, as written in the margin. In reality, the illustration shows the hill that stands at the foot of the mountain, clearly visible in the background. On the peak, in effect, it is possible to distinguish a square and regular shape that may well be all that survived of the structure.

According to the Bible, Aaron, during the passage through the desert, was unable to resist the demands of the people of Israel, and he had the golden calf set up and worshipped; for this reason, God did not allow him to enter the Promised Land and he died on Mount Hor, at the age of 123. His tomb, restored first by the Crusaders and later by the Muslims, is the destination of both Christian and Muslim pilgrims.

David Roberts R.A.

Tomb of AARON. Summit of Mount Hor. March 11th 1839.

Louis Haghe lith.

From David Roberts's journal:

12th - This morning we left at half-past 6, and proceeded towards Hebron. During the day we came upon an Arab encampment, with large flocks of sheep and goats. We bought a goat for about 35...
13th - Started this morning at 7. Our course still lay through the Wady El Ghor, or Wady Araba...

Mount Seir   Wady el Ghor.   March 4ᵗʰ 1839.

THE ENCAMPEMENT IN WADI ARABAH

Plate 36

12th-13th March 1839

*A*lthough they had already left the remarkable cliff city behind them several hours before, Roberts noted that for many miles around the slopes of the hills showed signs of terracing, the unmistakable indicators of a bygone era in which the entire region had been assiduously cultivated.

The night went by without any event, and they struck their tents at dawn; proceeding in the direction of Hebron along the Wadi El Ghor - also known as Wadi Arabah - Roberts and his fellow travellers encountered an Arab camp, around which grazed numerous flocks of sheep and herds of goats. The Beduin proved quite friendly, and many of the women gathered around the strangers to have a closer look at them. By common accord it was decided to spend the night there, and the tents were pitched in an area where there was abundant pasturage for the camels. The landscape, which consisted of limestone and jagged cliffs, seemed to be permeated with an air of melancholy; it all appeared grandiose in its savage desolation. On the following day, the 13th of March, Roberts and his entourage rose early and continued for a great many hours along the bed of the wadi, until they reached a well, surrounded by stands of reeds; the water, however, was stagnant and the camels refused to drink.

The travellers passed on. Towards midday, the caravan began to enter the hills to the left of the wadi, and they were soon able to slake their thirst with cool rainwater that had filled a small pool hidden amongst the rocks.

THE RUINS OF SEMUA

Plate 37

14th - 15th - 16th March 1839

*O*n the 14th of March, after breakfasting at the foot of the mountains that separate Wadi El Ghor from Judea, David Roberts and his travelling companions began the climb upward, which soon proved to be extremely tiring and steep, to the point that the trail at certain points became little more than a sort of stairway carved roughly into the living rock. At the top they found a number of ruins that Roberts was unable to identify as either Roman or Saracen. Once they had moved through

milk from the tribesmen, and after so many days of quenching his thirst with brackish water, he found the milk absolutely delightful.
Not far off, they saw the ruins of a tower or a fortress built on the brink of a deep gorge.
The buildings seem to have been crushed by an earthquake; Roberts was unable to learn the age or the origin of the construction. The entire region bracketed by Wadi Mousa and Hebron must once have been densely populated, but when Roberts was there, the

the pass, they finally began their descent into a valley of pleasant appearance, luxuriant and spangled with wildflowers.
The trail began to climb upward once again to the top of a hill. From there, they descended again to another valley not unlike the first, where a number of camels were grazing, the property of an Arab tribe. Roberts purchased some fresh

countryside and the villages appeared to be in a state of extreme neglect or, in many cases, to have been entirely abandoned. The village of Semua, as well, which was described in the Bible as a prosperous town, was now nothing more than a village of sheepherders. Roberts reached the place on the 16th of March, just before sighting Hebron.

Much of the population had left a few days earlier, taking their flocks with them, in search of new pastures but also - and chiefly - to flee conscription into the Egyptian army. In this illustration, Semua appears atop the hill, overshadowed by the massive ruins of a tower which may well have been part of fortifications dating back to Roman times.

From David Roberts's journal:

14th - After breakfasting at the foot of the mountains which separate Wady El Ghor from Judea, we commenced the ascent, which is very steep, the roadway being partly hewn in steps out of the rock... Overhanging a deep ravine, through which flows a stream, are the ruins of an ancient tower or fort, that seems to have been thrown down by an earthquake...

HEBRON

Plate 38

16th -17th -18th March 1839

*L*ocated in the heart of Judea, amidst a hilly landscape, Hebron is probably one of the oldest cities in the world, the site of ancient strife and impassioned devotion. Within the massive city walls built by King Herod, in fact, stands a church - later transformed into a mosque - which was built around 1195 atop the Cave of Makhpelah, where it is believed that Abraham, Isaac, Jacob, and their wives Sarah, Rebeccah, and Leah are buried. Hebrew tradition considers the tombs of the Patriarchs to be the legal foundation for the claim of the Jewish people to this territory. According to the Bible, this city was founded seven years before Tanis, that is, in the eighteenth century B.C., and it was near this city that the Biblical oak grove of Mamre stood, where Abraham lived.

The city was sacked by Joshua, and was the home of David - who was proclaimed King of Israel here - and the center of the revolt of Absalom. Rehoboam fortified the city, but it was destroyed by the Romans during the great revolt. Even after its destruction, however, the Jews never entirely abandoned it. The Crusaders, who called Hebron "Presidium Sancti Abrahe," designated the town an episcopal see in 1168; just twenty-one years later, however, the city fell back into the hands of the Muslims. The period of Mameluke rule constituted for the Jews a period of respite from persecution. Local lore has it that the prosperous business of manufacturing glass, in which Hebron still excels, was introduced by Venetian Jews, immediately following the Crusades.

David Roberts reached Hebron on the 16th of March 1839; he describes it as a city washed by sunlight, so peaceful and pleasant as to remind him of his native England. In particular, Roberts was impressed by the healthy appearance of the children, so different from the Egyptian children of the same age. The group of travellers received the hospitality of the only Christian family in the place, and set off again on the 18th, heading for Gaza. Having learned that an outbreak of the plague yet again prevented him from entering Jerusalem, the English artist decided very cheerfully to head for the coast and wait to see what would happen next.

From David Roberts's journal:

16th - Approaching Hebron, the hills are covered with vines and olive-trees. On turning round the side of a hill, Hebron first bursts upon you...
17th - To-day I made two coloured sketches of the town, but could not get admission to the mosque containing the tombs of Abraham, Isaac, and Jacob...

Beit Jibrin. March 7th 1839.

BETH GEBRIN

Plate 39

19th March 1839

From David Roberts's journal:

*19th - Left at daybreak, passing through
a richly cultivated country. About
sixteen miles from Hebron are the
remains of a castle, and Roman ruins,
consisting of a number of marble
columns. There is a village, which takes
its name from the Roman ruins and is
called Bed El Gebrin, the hous of
Gabriel...*

Roberts spent the night of the 18th of March in a small village called Terkumich, and by dawn of the next day he was back in the saddle. At a distance of about sixteen miles from Hebron, in the middle of a prosperous, well-tilled countryside, the small group of travellers stumbled upon the ruins of a Crusaders' castle and a number of ruins from Byzantine and Roman times, the lingering relics of the splendor of ancient Eleutheropolis. First known as Betogabra and later as Beit Gibrin - meaning the "abode of Gabriel - in A.D. 200, the city was raised to the Roman rank of municipium with the name of Eleutheropolis and was endowed with extensive lands. In the fourth century it was mentioned as a major episcopal see and as the capital of the province of southern Palestine. Around A.D. 315, the bishop Epiphanius was born there; he went on to become a prolific ecclesiastical author and to compile compendia of Christian doctrine. In A.D. 796, the region was caught up in a bloody civil war, and the city was razed to the ground. Three centuries later, the Crusaders built a fortress there to fend off attacks from the Saracens in the nearby Askelona. Later the place lost its strategic value and underwent a further and inexorable decline. In modern times, not far from what is now Beth Gebrin, extensive remains of monuments and a number of excellent mosaic floors from Byzantine times were found, perhaps the finest ever unearthed in Palestine. Roberts noted that he had admired a number of handsome Roman columns and the colossal foundations of a fortified complex, as well as a few splendid olive trees that looked to be quite old, and which were growing near the modest Arab village. The travellers set off again and toward sundown set up their tents in a place called Burier. That day, Roberts and his travelling companions had ridden for ten hours and were just two hours' ride from Gaza. It is worth noting here too that the date that appears in the margin of the illustration is certainly apocryphal.

GAZA

Plate 40

20th March 1839

The last stretch of road before Gaza wound through a region of luxuriant forests, broken here and there by fields of wheat and prosperous olive groves. Roberts considered the city to have an excellent location, spreading across a hilltop some two miles from the sea. A procession of sand dunes separated the city from the sea. Sadly, the city's ancient grandeur had been long ago broken into mere memories, and although it might seem quite imposing from a distance, the inhabitants appeared poverty-stricken. The city itself possessed no buildings worthy of any note. A great many of the houses and mosques, in fact, seem to have been built with fragments of far older structures, and indeed many shards of marble could be seen in the masonry. One miserable hut in particular captured Roberts's attention, since the roof was supported by splendid Roman capitals, piled one upon the other. Despite its humble appearance, the city did indeed boast a glorious past, made up of memorable events and an enviable wealth. It had been the capital of the nation of the Philistines and leading trading center, as well as the site of the legendary feats of Samson. Gaza was sacked by Ezekiah, and thereafter occupied repeatedly by Egyptians, Assyrians, Chaldeans, and Persians. Conquered in 332 B.C. by Alexander the Great and later by Ptolomey I, it was favored by the Romans, under whose rule it prospered as a trading center. Occupied by Crusaders in 1100, it saw them alternately victorious and beaten. In 1516 the Turks routed the Mamelukes there, and in 1799 the city was taken by Napoleon. When Roberts visited Gaza, it had a population of about fifteen thousand - five hundred of these being Christians. Today that population has tripled.

The city's destiny continues to be linked to its strategic location, and to a controversial and troubled history.

The troops which are clearly seen in this illustration were made up of two regiments of Egyptian Light Dragoons and Lancers, equipped and armed European-style, marching from Gaza to Sidon.

From David Roberts's journal:

20th - The approach to Gaza is through extensive forests. The city stands on a height two miles from the sea, from which it is sheltered by hills of sand. Its ancient grandeur is entirely gone; the inhabitants are wretchedly poor, and there are not even the ruins of any building of importance standing...

ASKELON

Plate 41

From David Robert's journal:

21st, 22nd, 23rd, and 24th - The port has been swept away, and the city is quite deserted. Ibrahim Pasha has caused a considerable portion to be excavated for stones to build a modern city...

21st - 22nd - 23rd March 1839

*T*he 21st of March and the following two days passed slowly, as the travellers waited for fresh camels in order to continue their voyage. After the long wait and despite the lengthy negotiations, Roberts was able to procure only five of the nine animals that he had requested. In any case, the Englishman was on his way again on the 23rd of March, dressed like a Turk once again. In the late afternoon, the group stopped in a small village called Burbah, not far from the place where the splendid Askelon had prospered in the distant past; this was the site of the love between Samson and Delilah. Once a capital of the Philistines, according to Greek mythology this town was founded by Ascalon, the son of Hymen, during the conquest of Syria. We have some documentation from Egyptian records that tell of Ascalon's rebellion against the rule of the pharaohs. The town is also mentioned in the Bible, and seems to have been noted more for the renowned products of its soil, than for the political events that occurred here.

The products mentioned are wine and scallion, a type of onion that takes its name from this town. The town came under Hebrew rule after the death of Joshua, and when the empire of Alexander the Great collapsed, it became part of the Kingdom of Egypt, then part of Syria, at which time it became the center of the cult of Astarte. An episcopal see during the early Christian era, it was still a flourishing town under Arab domination. During the Crusades, this was the site of bloody battles. It was destroyed by Saladin and rebuilt by Richard the Lion-Hearted; shortly thereafter it was abandoned once and for all.

It is now a major center of archeological research, and finds have been made here concerning the ancient civilizations that succeeded one another until the arrival of the Romans. Roberts notes that he found the city in a state of very grave neglect. The city walls were in ruins, the port facilities had virtually disappeared, and the entire zone inspired one with a great sense of desolation.

The only noteworthy features were the remains of a Corinthian temple, with columns still in place, and a large marble statue of a woman. Not far off stood an ancient Christian church that showed numerous elements of Greek Orthodox influence, including capitals adorned with a cross crowned with laurel.

Ashoood — March 24 1834

ASHDOD

Plate 42

David Roberts. R.A.

24th March 1839

Ashdod is today one of the most important commercial ports in Israel; it is located about twenty-five miles north of Askelon, not very far from Jaffa. David Roberts reached the place on the 24th of March, and at a first glance, it all appeared quite miserable, despite its excellent location in the midst of an exceedingly fertile countryside. The fact that the town lay along the major coast road seemed to Roberts to suggest a brighter future for the city which, in ancient times, had been one of the five leading cities of the civilization of the Philistines.

It was at Ashdod that the Ark of the Covenant was brought as booty of war after the defeat of the Jews; there the Ark was placed in the temple of Dagon, a pagan divinity in the form of a triton. The power of the Lord, however, was made manifest in a number of different episodes: first, the priests of the temple found the statue of the idol prostrate before the Ark. Then a terrible disease swept through the entire population. The Ark was then taken to the village of Gath, and then to the village of Ekron, but the pestilence continued to follow it. It was thus decided to give the Ark back to the Jews, and it was taken to Jerusalem by David as the supreme religious symbol of his reign.

JAFFA, SEEN FROM THE NORTH

Plate 43

25th March 1839

Breaking camp at the first light of dawn, Roberts and his fellow travellers first passed through a prosperous little town known as Ibrech, and quite soon thereafter from atop a hill that dominated the coastline, found themselves glimpsing the outskirts of Jaffa which was surrounded by orange groves. Roberts noted that the city, long ago known as Joppa, enjoyed a magnificent location. Southward, the eye could roam freely over the rich plains that extended toward Gaza, while northward the horizon was enclosed by the noble silhouette of Mount Carmel. To the east stretched the hills of Judea, toward Jerusalem, while to the west extended the endless waves of the Mediterranean. In the face of such natural magnificence, however, the narrow alleys of the city itself were a great disappointment. Disease and pestilence had devastated the population and a mere five thousand souls huddled in those white hovels amidst dust and poverty. Only from the outside did the city preserve its proud appearance, the heritage of a truly glorious past. According to Semitic legend, Jaffa was in fact founded by Japheth, the son of Noah. According to Greek mythology, the town was built by a daughter of Aeolus. It is also said that here Noah built his ark; that here Andromeda was left to the mercy of the sea monster; and that here Perseus washed the wounds he received in his battle with the Centaurs.

This was certainly the Joppa of the Philistines, burned by Judas Maccabee in the second century B.C., and later destroyed by Vespasian. The Arabs took the city in A.D. 637, but it was conquered twice by the Crusaders, until finally being expunged by the sultan Baibars and largely destroyed in 1267. The name of the city returned to the spotlight of history five centuries later in 1799 when it was occupied by Napoleon. At the time of Roberts's voyage, Jaffa had just fallen seven years earlier to Ibrahim, the son of Mohammed Ali, the pasha of Egypt. Today it forms part of the urban agglomeration of Tel Aviv and is a lively commercial center known throughout the world for its export of fruit and agricultural delicacies. The individuals in the foreground of this illustration are Polish Jews returning from their pilgrimage to Jerusalem, waiting to take passage back to Europe.

From David Roberts's journal:

25th - Leaving our encampment by daybreak, we passed a beautiful little town called Ibrech, and arrived at Jaffa, which is surrounded by orange groves, and stands on a hill sloping to the sea.

From David Roberts's journal:

26th - I examined the town carefully, but found very few antiquities.

Jaffa. March 26.ᵗʰ 1839.

JAFFA, SEEN FROM THE SOUTH

Plate 44

26th March 1839

*O*n the morning of the 26th, Kinnear bade Roberts farewell and set off for Beirut. Later that day, the English artist had an invitation to a reception at the consul's residence, where he was treated with great courtesy. The two chatted amiably and smoked a few pipes together. That same day, Roberts had wandered extensively through the town, without, however, finding any particular ancient monuments. In any case, Jaffa appeared to be a majestic and even spectacular city, set atop a sheer promontory that jutted out over the sea. This view from the north shows clearly how, due to the extreme steepness of the rough terrain, it was possible to see the entire town at a glance; many of the constructions, some of which were quite large, had foundations that covered several different stories, in a form of terracing, and long stretches of the streets were actually stairways. These features all gave the town a certain charming allure. All it lacked was trees or greenery of any sort, common though those may be in other major cities of the Middle East.

RAMLA, ANCIENT ARIMATHEA

Plate 45

oberts left Jaffa at ten in the morning on the 27th of March. He was accompanied by his friend John Pell, his guide Ishmael, and three servants.

The group of travellers had eight horses which bore tents and the remaining baggage. The road ran through the gardens and orchards that surround the city, and then crossed the plain of Sharon, well cultivated in the midst of that pleasant countryside, all a-flower and studded with small villages and palm groves. Roberts considered this to be some of the finest countryside he had ever seen. Around three o'clock in the afternoon, the travellers entered the town of Ramla, where they were welcomed joyfully by the Father Superior of the Latin convent. Later the same day the Father Superior accompanied him in a tour of the most ancient monuments in the village. What most caught the English artist's attention was the Great Mosque, which was said to be originally the church of the Knights of the Hospital of St. John of Jerusalem. Nonetheless, the structure clearly showed a strong Saracen influence, while the subterranean sections clearly included structures from the Roman era. Ramla, which remains a town with a predominantly Muslim culture, was founded by the Arabs around A.D. 716. During the Crusades it was often the site of battles, and it was occupied alternately by Christians and Egyptians. Richard the Lion-Hearted made his headquarters here. In 1276 it was

incorporated once and for all into the Kingdom of Egypt. It enjoyed a period of great prosperity under Turkish rule, and seemed immune to the general decline that laid low the other towns of the region, because of its excellent location on the great caravan route between Damascus and Egypt. In Ramla, which in Arabic means "sand," a great many immigrants of Balkan descent now live; there is also a sizable Arab community. Of particular interest are the White Mosque, the so-called Tower of the Forty, and the Great Mosque mentioned above, which was built on the ruins of a Crusaders' cathedral, as well as an interesting complex of underground cisterns dating back to the ninth century.

27th -28th March 1839

From David Roberts's journal:

27th - Left Jaffa at 9 A.M. for Jerusalem... Our way lay through the gardens which surround Jaffa, and across the plain of Sharon, through a richly-cultivated country. The ground is carpeted with flowers - the plain is studded with small villages and groups of palm-trees, and, independent of its interesting associations, the country is the loveliest I ever beheld. The mountains of Judea bound the view, and beyond is the Holy City. About 3 we arrived at Rameh, and were kindly received at the Latin Convent by the superior...

117

LOD, ANCIENT LYDDA

Plate 46

28th March 1839

*R*oberts spent the evening of the 27th of March at Ramla in the company of the monks of the convent, who had shown themselves in the meanwhile to be extremely jovial hosts. The following day the Englishman had a chance to visit the nearby town of Lod briefly. It had once been known by the name Lydda, and was supposedly the birthplace of St. George. In antiquity, it had been a busy local capital, the center of a complex network of roads, and a commercial center of considerable importance, mentioned in the documents of the Pharaohs as early as 1500 B.C. Later, it was united politically with Samaria, and later still with Judea, when it took part in the revolt against the Romans. The town was destroyed by Vespasian and by Hadrian, but it was rebuilt, and was dubbed Diospolis - or the "City of God" - by Septimius Severus. Lod became one of the earliest Christian communities, was an episcopal see under Constantine, but it declined as

Ramla prospered. Conquered by the Crusaders, who built a church in Frankish Romanesque style there and dedicated it to Saint George - the ruins of that church greatly impressed David Roberts - the city was destroyed by Saladin and bebuilt by Richard the Lion-Hearted. Sacked by the Mongols in 1271, it declined in importance until the modern day. Israel's national poet, Abraham Shlonski, has described it as the "city of Books, an oasis of peace and of watchtowers." After crossing the last hills of Judea, Roberts finally came within sight of the Holy City and spent the night camped just a short distance from the walls. In his journal, the English artist noted that the surrounding area was immersed in an absolute silence, broken only by the occasional howling of a distant dog and by the scream of a solitary owl, perched on the battlements. Here, too, the date that appears in the margin of the illustration should probably be moved up by a day or two.

Christian Church of St George at Lud

Lydda. March 29th 1839

David Roberts R.A.

JERUSALEM AND THE PILGRIMAGE
TO THE JORDAN RIVER

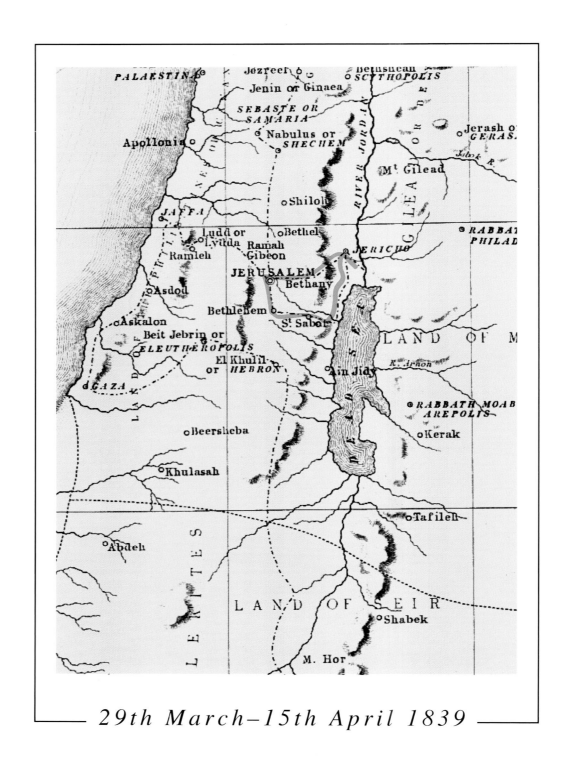

29th March–15th April 1839

David Roberts. R.A

The

HOLY LAND,

Syria, Idumea, Arabia, Egypt & Nubia.

FROM DRAWINGS MADE ON THE SPOT BY

David Roberts, R.A.

WITH HISTORICAL DESCRIPTIONS BY

THE REV.ᴰ GEORGE CROLY, L.L.D.

LITHOGRAPHED BY

LOUIS HAGHE.

VOL I.

LONDON, F. G. MOON, 20 THREADNEEDLE STREET,
PUBLISHER IN ORDINARY TO HER MAJESTY.
MDCCCXLII.

THE CITADEL OF JERUSALEM

Plate 47

29th March 1839

On the morning of the 29th of March, a Good Friday, the quarantine was finally lifted, and at long last Roberts was able to enter the city of Jerusalem; as he walked into the city, he saw the entire population thronging out of the city gates in a state of joyful celebration. Groups of soldiers marched to and fro, preceded by the pounding of the bass drum and by the brilliant colors of their military banners, followed by crowds of gleeful men, women, and children. Crowds of pilgrims pressed in from all sides, descending upon

of travellers made their way around the walls of Jerusalem, moving from the Damascus Gate toward Mount Zion. In all likelihood, this plate, which depicts the Citadel of Jerusalem, is based on the observations that Roberts made during that first excursion. The imposing fortified complex lies to the right of the Jaffa Gate, which is girt by a deep moat. On this site, around 24 B.C., Herod built three towers to protect his palace; these towers survived the destruction of Jerusalem ordered by Titus, and were subsequently turned into

Jerusalem for the Easter festivities; indeed, the British artist and his entourage had a difficult time finding accommodations. It was their extreme good luck to meet with Elias, the head of a large Christian family, who had received them in Hebron. Elias arranged for them to stay as the guests of his brother-in-law, an Orthodox Greek. In the course of the morning, the little group

barracks for the Twelfth Legion. During the Byzantine Era, this Citadel had fallen into such a state of disrepair that local anchorites had taken it over as a place of refuge and meditation. Rebuilt by the Crusaders, who garrisoned the place, the Citadel was destroyed once more at the hands of the Mamelukes in 1239 and lay in shattered ruins until 1335, a century later when the Turks rebuilt the fortress and

built atop the keep - still the most ancient part of the structure - one of their distinctive little minarets, now known as the Tower of David. Currently, the Citadel contains the Museum of the History of Jerusalem, which documents the many stages of the city's history; sound and light shows are held here during the evenings, providing an impressive spectacle.

Citadel of Jerusalem within the Walls

From David Roberts's journal:

29th, Good Friday - "It is better to be born lucky than rich" is an old proverb, and it applies to me. This morning the quarantine has been removed... I made the circuit of the city walls, proceeding northward by the gate of Damascus and the Valley of Jehoshaphat to the hill of Sion,

where the tomb of David is placed... After settling ourselves in our quarters we visited several interesting places, among others the Mosque of Omar, built near the pool of Bethesda, and the Holy Sepulchre, which is approached through a series of narrow streets, the last of which opens into a court...

THE ENTRANCE TO THE CITADEL OF JERUSALEM

Plate 48

29th March 1839

The walls of Jerusalem, with the Citadel on their western side, boast an extremely complex history, the faithful mirror of the military fortunes of the city over the course of the centuries. The circuit of walls as they stand today, extending over a circumference of roughly two and a half miles, is certainly much smaller than the walls that must have girded the city of Zion prior to the second destruction of the temple at the orders of Emperor Titus. Even Aelia Capitolina, which Emperor Hadrian had rebuilt on the ruins of the Jewish city, occupied a smaller area. Presumably, the walls built by Hadrian served their function until the time of the Crusades, although the city by that time had expanded far beyond that perimeter.

The structure of the walls must have presented some quite evident signs of wear and damage; in fact, in 1178 they underwent extensive repair. Nine years later, Saladin nonetheless managed to overcome the resistance of the city's defenders and took Jerusalem. Victorious though the new conqueror may have been, he still feared the desire for revenge from Richard the Lion-Hearted. Saladin worked tirelessly to ensure that the walls should be reinforced and, where necessary, rebuilt from the foundations up. Six months of hard work, with Saladin himself lending a hand, made Jerusalem an impregnable fortress. By a fluke of destiny, in 1219, the Sultan of Damascus, Melek, fearing that the city might fall into the hands of the Christians and become a dangerous enclave in his realm, ordered that the entire ring of walls be destroyed, with the sole exceptions of the Citadel and the Noble Enclosure. In 1229, without an arrow fired or a sword drawn, a treaty was drawn handing over Jerusalem to the Holy Roman Emperor Frederick II of Swabia. It stipulated that the walls of the city could not be rebuilt. Ten years later, however, the new rulers of Jerusalem felt threatened and reinforced the walls with the help of Pisan master builders. The new walls and turrets could do little to staunch the might of the emir Kerek, who pierced Jerusalem's defenses, massacred all the Latins, and dismantled the entire complex of fortifications. In 1243, a new treaty handed over the city to the Christians, who immediately set out to reinforce the walls. The next year, the Crusaders lost the Holy City for once and all, trounced by an Islamic military coalition. It was not until 1542 that the ring of walls was newly rebuilt, and this time, the walls survived. It is no accident, however, that the structures that now stand possess a number of heterogeneous and alien features, in some cases dating back from Roman times, and in other cases, from the reign of Solomon.

THE GOLDEN GATE

Plate 49

29th March 1839

The eastern walls of the city, at the foot of which lies a Muslim cemetery, are broken by the elegant forepart of the Golden Gate, which Roberts was able to admire during his walk around the walls. The fortification stands several yards higher than the surrounding countryside, and was rebuilt during the Byzantine era on the ruins of a Roman tower from the reign of Hadrian. The lower section of the walls and the vaults of the two twin arches seem to belong to the original structure, which has been renovated and modified extensively over the centuries. The Crusaders expanded and embellished them during their rule over Jerusalem, and the sultan Suleiman the Magnificent had them restored in the sixteenth century, when he incorporated them into the circuit of walls that even today surrounds the Old City.

The Golden Gate, also known as the Gate of Mercy, had been walled up as early as the conquest by the Crusaders, but it was opened once a year, during Palm Sunday, since tradition held that Jesus passed through here during his entrance into the Temple. Nonetheless, it was definitively sealed in 1530 by the Muslims, who even kept a squadron of guards here in the fear of the prophecy that the new king of Jerusalem and of the entire world would enter the city through that very gate.

Even now, many believe that the Golden Gate will miraculously be reopened only when the Messiah enters for the second time the city of David.

Mosque of Omar Shewing the Site of the Temple

THE MOSQUE OF OMAR

Plate 50

29th March 1839

After settling into his new accommodations, Roberts elaborated on his first and cursory tour of the city, going to see the most interesting sights. Among these sights was the celebrated Mosque of Omar, which, perched atop Mount Moriah, dominates the skyline of Jerusalem. Here, on the flat space known as the Noble Enclosure, stood the Second Temple, which Titus destroyed. Following the Arab conquest, Caliph Omar built a small wooden mosque here as a mark of devotion. Jerusalem is sacred to the Muslims because of the magical Night Journey that the Prophet Mohammed supposedly made to the city from Mecca. After reaching the Temple Mount, the Prophet Mohammed went to the sacred rock upon which, according to the Bible, Abraham was about to sacrifice his son, Isaac, when the Angel stayed his hand. On the same night, God transported Mohammed back to Mecca - this story establishes the Prophet's descent from Abraham. Rebuilt around A.D. 699 by Caliph Abd al-Melik, the Mosque of Omar, also known as the Dome of the Rock, is one of the sacred places of Islam. The splendid gilt dome covers the rock of Abraham, and there a footprint carved into the rock marks the spot from which Mohammed departed for heaven. A masterpiece of Arabic art, the Mosque of Omar glitters with gold and ceramics. Panels of multicolored majolica and strips bearing inscriptions from the Koran adorn the upper portion of the building, while the lower part of the building, octagonal in shape, is covered with marble panels with delicate pastel shades. The pilgrims in the foreground of the illustration are shown on the terrace that stands before the church of St. Anne; at the bottom of the gorge behind them is the Pool of Bethesda.

The Church of the Holy Sepulchre

Plate 51

29th March 1839

*A*s soon as Roberts reached Jerusalem, he received a warm welcome from the governor of the city, Achmet Aga, whose residence was said to be located on the exact spot where the palace of Herod had once stood. This was the beginning, moreover, of the Via Dolorosa, which wends its tortuous way to the Holy Sepulchre. The route is punctuated by a number of "stations," which supposedly correspond to the various episodes recounted in the Gospels in reference to Jesus's painful climb to Calvary and His subsequent Crucifixion. While the entire Via Dolorosa was of considerable interest,

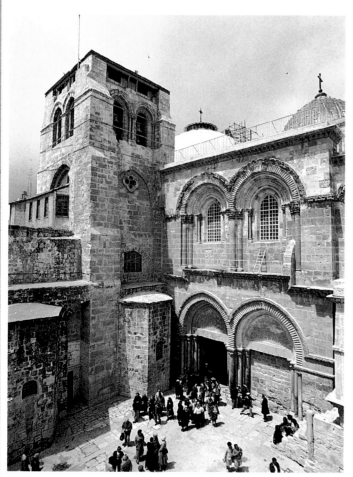

as it wound through the narrow streets of the most ancient part of the city, Roberts was keenly aware that the expectations of the faithful might be disappointed at the nearly shabby and certainly unimpressive appearance of the Holy Sepulchre itself. The area that stood before the monument, in fact, was crowded with miserable and tumbledown shacks; at the time of Roberts's visit, the square was used as a sort of bazaar, where a busy trade thrived in sacred images and relics. The English artist noted in his travel journal that with the possible exception of the facade, the exterior of the Holy Sepulchre possessed absolutely no noteworthy features, and appeared nothing more than a jumbled clutter of mismatched elements.

This appearance was without a

Church of the Holy Sepulchre Jerusalem

doubt in part the product of the necessity of crowding together under one roof all of the fundamental passages of the Passion of Christ. Despite its lack of architectural unity, the Holy Sepulchre remains one of the fundamental sacred monuments in Jerusalem and of all Christendom, for centuries a lightning rod for the faith and emotions of pilgrims who, although of many different confessions, gathered here to pray side by side. The church was founded in A.D. 326; tradition has it that Queen Helena, the mother of Constantine, was for founding the church. She is said to have believed that the church marked the exact site of Golgotha. The original structure of the church, however, was destroyed in A.D. 614, and the current appearance of the Holy Sepulchre dates largely from the Crusades, although major renovation was carried out by the Greek Orthodox monks following the fire of 1808. Inside the Holy Sepulcher, a rotunda stands above the tomb of Christ and, not far away, a chapel has been built on what is believed to be the exact point where the Virgin Mary discovered that her son had been resurrected.

Stone of Unction,
Holy Sepulchre.

THE STONE OF UNCTION

Plate 52

30th March 1839

Most of the sites sacred to Christianity are "jointly held" by a number of religions. There was a time when this co-existence was far from brotherly, and at times ferocious disputes ensued concerning the varied array of rights and jurisdictions. Nowadays, however, it seems that an increasingly ecumenical spirit is spreading. Quite heterogeneous in architectural terms, the Church of the Holy Sepulchre is now under the direct administration of Franciscan monks, with the assistance of Greek Orthodox monks, as well as Copts, and Armenians. Each of the Christian communities runs its own chapels and altars, celebrating their rituals according to different, rigidly planned-out schedules; moreover, each confession oversees the work of restoration of its own sector. In Jerusalem, the religions seem in any case to be complementary one to another, rather than being antagonists in a welter of liturgies and liturgical garb unequalled anywhere else on earth. This predisposition to tolerance, so fundamental to the peaceful coexistence of different ethnic groups, was fostered as far back as during the Ottoman rule. Adherents to moderate policies in the field of religion, and particularly sensitive to the economic benefits to be derived from the regular flow of Christian pilgrims, the Turks never hindered religious functions or restricted access to the Holy Sepulchre. Because of this cannily tolerant behavior, Roberts was able to tour the church quite freely. Inside the church, he depicted with an acutely observant eye the professions of faith being made upon the Stone of Unction. Tradition has it that this unadorned slab of white marble serves to protect the underlying slab of pink limestone, upon which the body of Christ, after the Deposition from the Cross, was sprinkled with myrrh and aloe by Joseph of Arimathea and Nicodemus, and that as it lay upon the slab of pink limestone, the Virgin Mary wept over it before the burial. Even today, the Stone of Unction is lighted by numerous oil lamps and adorned by silver candelabra, smaller nowadays than those that were portrayed by the English artist - back then the candelabra stood about six and a half feet tall. The lamps that can be seen in the plate were gifts from Greek Orthodox, Latin, and Armenian convents, whose monks back then took turns in overseeing the running of the church.

Roberts's journal informs us that on the Saturday in question, the 30th of March, the governor of Jerusalem had invited Roberts to make use of the upper floors in his residence in order to sketch some views of the city.

THE ENTRANCE TO THE TOMBS OF THE KINGS

Plate 53

31st March 1839

On Palm Sunday, after witnessing the procession to the Holy Sepulchre led by the Greek Orthodox archbishop, Roberts visited the Valley of Jehosaphat for the first time. Here, not far from the Damascus Gate, stands the so-called Tombs of the Kings. The actual burial chamber, carved into the limestone wall of the hill, and quite similar to the rock-cut structures of Petra, appears as a deep niche cut in the form of a portal, about twenty-six feet in width.

On either side, two pillars must once have stood, while the same number of columns - which served to support the massive architrave - have evidently been destroyed or lost.

The architrave is decorated with an elegant fascia of floral motifs, now badly damaged; above this strip is a decoration made of metopes and triglyphs and a high cornice. The entire decorative complex clearly reflects the influence of Imperial Roman style.

The space that is marked off by the portal leads to a deep antechamber carved out of the living rock; behind it there are three large burial chambers and two smaller ones.

Here Roberts was able to admire the fragmentary remains of a number of marble sarcophagi, whose excellent reliefs seemed to him to be the only surviving documentation of ancient Hebrew art.

Although the burial chamber was long believed to be the final resting place of a number of kings of Israel, it is far more likely that this is the tomb of Helena Adiabene, a queen of Mesopotamia who converted to Judaism.

From David Roberts's journal:

March 31st, Palm Sunday - To-day splendid processions, in which the Greek Christians took precedence; and led by their bishops, they walked three times round the Sepulchre, bearing branches of palm in commemoration of Christ's entry into Jerusalem. The bishops, ascending the steps to the altar, blessed the multitude. A plenteous supply of holy water was distributed and flowers were strewn on the steps leading to the Sepulchre. Other Christian sects followed, all animated by sincere veneration. Visited the tombs of the three kings of Judea...

JERUSALEM, SEEN FROM THE ROAD TO BETHANY

Plate 54

The governor of Jerusalem, above and beyond his kind welcome to David Roberts and companions, told the artist that within a few days he would personally be escorting a caravan of Christian pilgrims to the banks of the Jordan, and he invited Roberts to come along. The governor offered to give Roberts mounts and a few armed guards, against all events. The trip was to take no more than a week, and in the meanwhile, they could visit the shores of the Dead Sea, Jericho, Bethlehem, and the famous cliff convent of St. Saba.

Roberts happily accepted the invitation and began to prepare for the departure. The caravan set out on the first of April in the early morning hours; after crossing the Valley of Jehosaphat and climbing the slopes of the Mount of Olives, they were soon in sight of the village of Bethany, which is just less than two miles from Jerusalem. Although the illustration is clearly dated the 5th April 1839, it should be placed in the earliest part of the trip. The journal tells us in fact that on the 5th of April David Roberts was already in Bethlehem.

Here, too, we should presume that the plate was not dated by the author and that it was erroneously dated by Louis Haghe or by one of his colleagues just before going to press. At the center of this view,

drawn from high atop the Mount of Olives, it is possible to recognize the Mosque of Omar, while to the left is the Mosque of El Aksa.

The depression which begins at the foot of the hill, crossed by the small stream of the Kidron, is the Valley of Jehosaphat, in which it is possible to make out the white tip of the tomb of Absalom.

From David Roberts's journal:

April 1st - Having got horses, left for Jericho, taking with me my portmanteau, tent, and servant. Crossing the Valley of Jehoshaphat, and ascending the Mount of Olives, we passed close to Bethany, the principal object in which is a building like a sheikh's tomb, called the House of Lazarus...

1st April 1839

BETHANY

Plate 55

1st April 1839

Bethany is mentioned in the Gospel as the home of Lazarus and of his two sisters, Mary and Martha.
It was in this small village at the gates of Jerusalem that Jesus supposedly performed the miracle of resurrection.
It is to this remarkable event that Bethany owes its fame and also its modern name, El Azarieh, which is Arabic for "Lazarus." Despite the sacred nature of the place, Bethany looked to David Roberts like a rundown conglomeration of miserable huts, many of which were built with material taken from ancient ruins. No more than a few dozen families lived in the town. Then as now, popular lore indicates with great certainty the houses in which

Mary, Martha, and Simon the Leper once lived, and of course, the tomb of Lazarus.
The sepulchre in question, which can be easily recognized in the illustration by Roberts, is the small square building topped by a dome to the left of the town itself; in reality it is a deep niche carved into the limestone and can be reached along a steep stairway.
The site was already a place of worship in early Christian times, and the earliest documented mention of it dates from A.D. 333. Seventy years later, St. Jerome describes it as being covered by a church, and in subsequent centuries, a number of monasteries and other sacred buildings were constructed there.

David Roberts R. A   Bethany april 1st 1839

THE DESCENT UPON THE VALLEY OF THE JORDAN

Plate 56

1st April 1839

From Bethany onward, the road that drops away toward Jericho wends its way through a highly unusual landscape, where neither houses nor plowed fields interrupt the monotonous succession of hills, each as bare and brightly colored as the last and the next, a surreal procession of sun-bleached peaks, among which the track curved and wound as if in a labyrinth, in the bed of arid valleys that seem never to have known the gurgle of water or the presence of any living creatures. An absolute silence, broken only by the stirring of the wind and the rattle of pebbles tumbling down the steep slopes of the hills - this silence weighed down upon the pilgrims, amplifying the terrors of the voyage.

Indeed, this territory was sadly famous for the raids of desert brigands, and the last mountain pass was particularly feared. This illustration shows that last pass, and the spectacular panorama that greeted the travellers after they had made their way through it.

The Jordan Valley, the silvery line of which is barely visible, lay spread out under the fading light of sunset. The glittering surface of the Dead Sea shone on the right, while the brightly colored tents of the pilgrims could be seen in the distance. In the presence of such spectacular beauty, Roberts observed that the scene was more suited to the pen of a poet than to the pencil of an artist. Although the great depression of the Dead Sea is one of the most arid places on the planet, it should be noted that around the southern course of the Jordan River and in the area surrounding Jericho, the presence of numerous springs makes the land remarkably fertile; the English artist, in fact, observed this in his journal.

From David Roberts's journal:

April 1st - Proceeding along the road, which has been all pavemented by the Romans, we first beheld the Dead Sea. Along the whole line, Arab horsemen and Bedouins were stationed. Groups of pilgrims were moving on to the Jordan. On our left is a brawling stream, at the bottom of a deep ravine, the sides of which are perforated with caves, the former abodes of anchorites. Farther on is a pool and stream, said to be that sweetened by Elisha. Jericho lies at the base of the hills...

Encampment of Pilgrims Jericho April 1st 1839

THE ENCAMPMENT OF PILGRIMS

Plate 57

1st April 1839

*I*n the Gospel according to St. Mark, it is written: "And it came to pass in those days, that Jesus came from Nazareth of Galilee, and was baptized of John in Jordan." It is therefore not hard to understand why over the centuries multitudes of the faithful have ventured to undertake the difficult and perilous journey to bathe and purify themselves, during the Easter time, in the waters of the river, not far from Jericho. And so it happened that in April of 1839 David Roberts was able to produce another one of his early "scoops"; during this period, the entire territory was plagued by the raids of robber brigands, and the caravans of pilgrims usually travelled with the escort of a considerable troop of armed guards, provided by the governor of Jerusalem. This strange mixture of the power of faith and the necessity of weapons can be found even now at Allenby Bridge, just a few miles from the site of the Baptism of Christ, a sensitive crossroads of many different cultures and faiths. Roberts, who until then had travelled with the protection of armed men put at his disposal by Achmet Aga, was finally greeted by Achmet Aga himself, while still in the vicinity of Jericho. Later, the artist noted in his notebook that he had been received, with exquisite courtesy, in the tent of the high official, who had offered him sherbets and coffee. Towards evening, the two men rode together to the banks of the Jordan, where preparations were already under way for the following day. The scene that Roberts portrayed here was remarkably lively. The camp is dominated by the tent of the governor; all around the tent, numerous groups of pilgrims are busily engaged in various activities. A number of horsemen ride their horses at a gallop, while other men from the escort chat idly. In the background is the motionless surface of the Dead Sea.

Bankes of. The Jordan . April 2nd 1839 .

THE IMMERSION IN THE JORDAN RIVER

Plate 58

2nd April 1839

On the morning of the 2nd of April, the pilgrims set out once again. Later, a cannon shot indicated that the governor too had set off. The caravan stretched out of sight, and the silence of the desert was barely disturbed by the shuffling tramp of all those feet. Nonetheless, as soon as the banks of the Jordan appeared in the near distance, the crowd set off at a mad dash, while women launched shrill shrieks of joy, not unlike those that Roberts had already noted in Egypt. At this point the governor's men arranged a number of carpets and comfortable chairs upon a promontory that overlooked the waters. Achmet Aga took a seat there, and his soldiers began patrolling.

Under the rather curious eyes of David Roberts, women and men began to strip and, in a remarkable display of a total lack of inhibition, they ventured out into the rapid current of the Jordan that runs at that point between sheer cliffs sunk deep below the plain of Jericho. Many of the faithful were entirely naked, while others wore light garments that they would later take home with them, religiously preserving them for the day of their own funerals. Unfortunately, a young Greek was drowned in the treacherous waters of the river and a number of other imprudent pilgrims ran the same risk, as they had ventured out too far into the current. The entire ceremony lasted only a couple of hours until the pilgrims lined up on the route home with the governor bringing up the rear of the procession.

In this illustration, Achmet Aga and his men can be clearly distinguished in the foreground.

From David Roberts's journal:

April 2nd - I was very much struck with the breadth of the plain of Jericho, and the narrow space in which the deep and rapid stream is cooped up between the steep banks. The scene in the river was most exciting. Young and old, male and female, were in the stream in one promiscuous mass...

THE ENCAMPMENT NEAR JERICHO

Plate 59

Situated to the north of the Dead Sea, the city of Jericho boasts an extremely ancient history. According to the Bible, Joshua conquered the city, apparently around the thirteenth century B.C. During Roman times, it was endowed with sumptuous palaces built by Herod the Great, and it later became an episcopal see during the Christian era. After the Crusades, a slow but ineluctable decline began, which David Roberts clearly witnessed during his brief visit. The town appeared to him to be little more than a heap of ruins, a few miserable huts surrounded by small pens for the domestic animals, dominated by the remains of a Saracen tower, somewhat loftily described as the Castle. The few inhabitants farmed a remarkably fertile land, rich in palm trees and vineyards, although the air was heavy and overheated, almost seeming to crush the horizon under a mantle of silence. Roberts had passed through here upon his way to the River Jordan, and he passed through here again at dawn on the 3rd of April, while on his way to the Monastery of St. Saba.
This illustration shows an encampment of Beduins, who spent the night not far from the tower of Jericho. Under the silvery rays of a full moon, the surface of the Dead Sea appears smooth, luminous, and unshadowed. Swimming in the pale light of the moon, the desolation of the surrounding desert touches the realm of pure poetry, while the deep and brackish Dead Sea sheds any sense of its harsh three-dimensional reality, until it mutates into an imaginary landscape. This illustration by Roberts contrasts sharply with the image of modern-day Jericho, a luxuriant oasis of bougainvilleas and orange groves. Recent digs have transformed this into one of the most interesting archeological attractions in the region.

3rd April 1839

THE WILDERNESS SURROUNDING ST. SABA

Plate 60

3rd April 1839

Convent of S. Saba. April 1839.

After taking his leave of Achmet Aga, who had provided him the evening before with guides who knew the area well, Roberts left the plain of Jericho in the early hours of the 3rd of April. At first the road ran along the foot of the highlands, and the group of horsemen rode along with the waters of the Dead Sea on their left. Three hours later, Roberts and his companions made a stop near a spring of drinkable water. A little further along, the coast turned into a scarp and the group of travellers was forced to climb along a very steep trail, which became quite dangerous in certain stretches, winding as it did along the sheer drop into the depression.

This enormous effort was repaid by the remarkable view that they had from the top of the mountain: the surface of the Dead Sea, smooth as enamel, glittered like a mirror, and reflected the surrounding hills. In that motionless and evocative silence, no one in the little group said a word.

They descended along the Fire Valley. Wadi el Naar, in the local tongue, was equally arduous and full of strange allure. Once they had passed the stream of the Kidron, which here runs between equally sheer banks, the group proceeded for a distance along a rough and uneven ground, largely made up of reddish limestone, where an unusually luxuriant vegetation grew. At some distance, they finally glimpsed the towers of the Monastery of St. Saba, a remarkable complex of buildings perched on the walls of the remarkable canyon of the Kidron.

Roberts was so impressed by the spectacle that he wrote in his journal that he could not imagine a more romantic setting.

149

THE DEAD SEA FROM THE HIGHLAND OF EIN GEDI

Plate 61

4th April 1839

This view of the Dead Sea, dated 4th April 1839, was sketched from high atop Ein Gedi, not far from the monastery of St. Saba, which appears here in all its astounding drama and impressiveness, perched high atop the cliff carved out by the Kidron. The Dead Sea, some fifty miles in length and eleven miles in width at its widest, lies in the deepest tectonic ditch carved out of the earth's surface, at about one thousand two hundred and ninety-six feet below sea level. This surrealistic body of water is surrounded by an extremely arid landscape on both sides, and only in the northern extremity, near the mouth of the Jordan, does the humidity permit some scattered vegetation to survive. Never brushed by the humid breezes that make the area to the west of Jerusalem so fertile, ten times saltier than any other sea on earth, and so dense that it is impossible to dive into its waters, the Dead Sea has no outlet and has no life forms. Amidst such arid desolation - which struck Roberts however as being rich in mystery and majesty - the occasional oasis appears as an improbable mirage, the guardian of a life that is here negated by the hostility of the land and the pitiless glare of the sun. With its freshwater springs and its luxuriant greenery, Ein Gedi attracted the English artist with all the power of an unexpected miracle.

The Dead Sea,
looking towards Moab
April 4th 1839

Convent of St Saba April 4 1839

David Roberts R.A.

THE CONVENT OF ST. SABA

Plate 62

4th April 1839

*B*uilt against the stark rock walls of the gorge dug out by the Kidron River as it flows toward the Dead Sea, the Monastery of St. Saba is a place set aside for isolation and prayer amidst the silent desolation of the desert, a few miles southeast of Jerusalem. Founded in A.D. 492, but destroyed by the Arabs during the seventh century, the Monastery was quickly rebuilt in a radical new version; John of Damascus was ordained a priest here, and he wrote his fundamental theological treatises here. The architectural complex, whose most noteworthy features are the cupolas, painted bright blue, and the enormous enclosure wall, is clearly a piece of defensive construction; the walls are very thick and are well arrayed, the windows are little more than loopholes, and the entrances are narrow and low, and are girded with stout portals. Inside, the relics of St. Saba are preserved; they were brought here from Venice in 1965, after being held there for more than seven centuries. As it was when David Roberts toured it, the Monastery is now run by Greek Orthodox monks, who forbid women from entering there. In Roberts's journal, his first view of and approach to this remarkable monument is described in terms of hushed wonder: aside from the inevitable considerations on the remarkable architecture of the place, the English artist notes that he was pleasantly surprised at the cordial hospitality of the monks and at the astonishing comforts the Monastery yielded. Walls and floors were covered with thick carpets, the air was cool and healthful, and the local wine - made from grapes perhaps harvested from terraces dug into the rocky wall - was pleasing to the palate.

From David Roberts's journal:

April 3rd - The convent consists of a cluster of buildings on the face of the rock, and contains many chapels. The brotherhood is of the Greek persuasion, and numbers about thirty-five monks, who dress the same as those of Mount Sinai.
4th and 5th - On looking from the heights above down on the convent, one could scarcely believe that it could possess so many comforts and conveniences within its walls...

THE CHAPEL OF THE CONVENT OF ST. SABA

Plate 63

5th April 1839

Chapel of the Convent of St. Saba.
April 5th 1839.

*T*he day after his arrival at St. Saba, David Roberts asked for and received permission to sketch the chapel of the Monastery of St. Saba. With great courtesy, the monks even allowed the artist to complete his work after the religious services had begun. The setting, quite ancient, was heavily decorated in adherence to the ornate style found in so many Greek Orthodox churches. One of the frescoes, which depicts Judgment Day, was the object of particular devotion, while figures of saints adorned virtually the entire surface of the pillars. Just prior to David Roberts's visit, the Russian government, which was particularly sensitive to the welfare of Orthodox churches throughout the Middle East, had sent a huge number of very fine icons to St. Saba, and had also paid for the restoration of the entire building and its adjacent structures. Around noon on the 5th of April, the travellers bid the monks farewell, having left an offering for other, penniless travellers who might happen that way. They then set off for Bethlehem, which they reached after a three-hour ride.

BETHLEHEM

Plate 64

Bethlehem lies about five miles from Jerusalem, amidst countryside that yields such rich harvests that the area's original name was "Ephrata," or "fertile." Despite the historical prestige of the village, mentioned in ancient Hebrew history as the native home of the family of David, who was probably born there, it boasts no monuments or urban grandeur. Most texts describe the town as small and unassuming.

Modesty and poverty fit well, after all, with the character of the Savior; evangelistic tradition, in fact, has it that Bethlehem was the birthplace of Jesus Christ, who was born in a cave there, according to St. Jerome. It quickly became one of the holy places of Christianity, and the destination of endless pilgrimages. As so often happens in the Holy Land, where history and religion overlap in a setting found nowhere else on earth, Bethlehem is not sacred only to Christians: the Jewish religion also holds the village sacred to the memory of Rachel, wife of the Patriarch Jacob, and archetype of the suffering of all Jewish mothers. Her tomb, just outside of the village, is the object of great veneration because it is considered a symbol of the redemption of Israel. David Roberts arrived in Bethlehem in the afternoon of the 5th of April. Scrupulous as ever, he writes in his journal that he encountered a great many flocks of sheep during his trip to St. Saba, and that the immediate outskirts of the village seemed quite fertile, with fields of wheat broken here and there by olive groves or fig trees.

From David Roberts's journal:

April 5th - The Church of the Nativity crowns the height on which the town is situated, and around it are the Latin, Greek, and Armenian convents. The Church of the Nativity is in form similar to the Basilica at Rome, with a double row of Corinthian columns supporting a wall, above which rises a timber roof. The wall is covered with scriptural subjects, most elaborately executed in mosaic, but much mutilated...

THE CHURCH OF THE NATIVITY

Plate 65

6th April 1839

From the hills surrounding the city, David Roberts observed that the landscape of Bethlehem is dominated by the hill upon which stands the Church of the Nativity, which is probably one of the oldest churches on earth. It was built at the orders of St. Helena, the mother of the Emperor Constantine, around A.D. 330. The church was restored and partly renovated as early as the sixth century at the orders of Justinian who, it was said, reduced the height of the doors in order to prevent the sacrilegious from entering the church on horseback. In 1479, lastly, the beams of the ceiling were replaced, thanks to the generosity of all the leading Kingdoms of Christendom. The building presents the architectural characteristics of the Roman basilica, and is reminiscent of the church of Saint Paul in Rome; the interior, which is divided into five naves by Corinthian columns and pilasters made of yellow marble, appears sumptuously ornate. Over long centuries of pilgrimage, in fact, the faithful of all the denominations of Christianity have left their mark, in a blaze of votive lamps and icons distinctive to each confession. In this connection, Roberts noted in his journal that the interior of this church is strictly divided into different areas of jurisdiction: while the choir is occupied by the so-called Greek Orthodox Church, the arms of the transept - beneath which lies the Shrine of the Nativity - are instead occupied by the Latin Chapel and the Armenian Chapel. The beginning of the dispute among the three different Christian churches over who rightly possessed the sanctuary dates back to the sixteenth century, but even today the church is surrounded by the convents of the three religious communities, which take turns in officiating at the ecclesiastical rites and ceremonies.

THE SHRINE OF THE NATIVITY

Plate 66

6th April 1839

The Shrine of the Nativity, where Greek Orthodox monks now officiate, is a small and cramped space, its walls partially sheathed in marble yet quite stark when compared with the opulence usually found in Greek Orthodox churches.
In a small apse, the altar of the Nativity of Christ, is adorned with fifteen silver lamps - symbolizing the various denominations of Christianity - and with a silver star, marking the point where Jesus is though to have been born. Upon the star, which represents the comet sighted by the Magi, a Latin inscription explains simply: "Hic De Virgine Maria Jesus Christus Natus Est." Along the sides of the grotto, one after the other, are two small altars: one is the altar of the Manger, in which the Infant Jesus was laid for a crib, the other is the altar of the Magi, who came here to adore the Christ Child.
Tradition has it that the original Manger, brought to Rome at the orders of Pope Sixtus V, is now found in a side chapel of Santa Maria Maggiore. David Roberts writes that, just as he was drawing the interior of the Shrine, a man arrived from Jerusalem carrying the sacred flame; immediately all of the Greek Orthodox faithful clustered around the herald in order to light their lamps at the flame of divine origins.
Roberts's drawing emphasizes the many oil lamps, left as gifts by Christian pilgrims, which then softened the setting with their gentle light, as they do today.

160

Jerusalem, from the Mount of Olives

Plate 67

7th-8th April 1839

On the way back from Bethlehem, on the 7th of April, Roberts wrote that he rode on horseback as far as the so-called Pools of Solomon, which supplied drinking water for the residents of Jerusalem, and which he believed to have been constructed by the Saracens. The following morning, John Pell left the group of travellers and started back to Cairo, and shortly afterwards Roberts returned to Jerusalem. Although the artist writes in his diary that he wandered through the Valley of Jehosaphat and that he had explored the rock-cut tombs that are found here, and which can be seen in the following illustrations - this plate is also dated 8th April. It is therefore quite likely that the drawing - a view of Jerusalem from the top of the Mount of Olives in which it is possible to descry quite clearly the Tomb of Absalom - was executed the morning Roberts returned to the city. The Biblical David came to this long-venerated site to seek refuge, after surviving the revolt instigated by Absalom. At the foot of the Mount is the Garden of Gethsemane, where Jesus was betrayed. In the cemeteries that extend along the slopes of the Mount, thousands of Jews and pilgrims are buried because it is here, according to the Prophets, that the dead will be resurrected. The view created by Roberts shows the eastern quarter of Jerusalem; at the very center lies the Noble Enclosure, where a mosque was built to protect the Rock, from which Mohammed ascended to heaven.

THE TOMB, OF ZECHARIAH

Plate 68

The Valley of Qidron , which winds between the Temple Mount and the Mount of Olives, and which is also known as the Valley of Jehosaphat, features numerous remains of ancient settlements. The upper portion of the valley, with its harsh slopes dotted here and there by small patches of vegetation, was used as a burial ground even in ancient times. Four monumental tombs still stand in good condition. Two of these tombs - that of Jehosaphat and that of St. James - are made of architectural carved into the rocky cliff wall; behind them are the crypts proper. The of Absalom and of Zechariah,

on the other hand, are authentic monumental structures, carved in a single block from the side of the mountain. Despite their clearly Biblical names, these two surprising funerary structures date from Hellenistic times, and once formed part of a vast necropolis in which wealthy and well-to-do citizens from the court of Herod were buried. The correct attribution of the tomb of Zechariah is difficult to

be ascertained, as it is not known whether the Zechariah in question was the prophet - who is said to be buried elsewhere - or Zechariah, the father of John the Baptist. The monument is formed of a cube, some twenty feet to a face, and entirely detached from the slope of the hill.

The faces of the cube are punctuated by half-columns with Ionic capitals and corner pillars. The cornice above, which presents elegant motifs of acanthus leaves, terminates in a jutting molding. Atop the molding is an obtuse pyramid just about ten feet in height. The tomb - which rises on a base made up of three tall stairs, beneath which is the entrance to the burial chamber - was partly buried until the beginning of this century. Roberts, in fact, depicted it as a striking form emerging from the sand.

It is interesting to observe that popular tradition holds that not far from the Tombs of the Prophets is the place where the souls will be weighed on Judgment Day, in preparation for the Resurrection of the Flesh.

8th April 1839

THE TOMB OF ST. JAMES

Plate 69

A *few yards to the left of the Tomb of Zechariah, and carved out of the same rocky cliff, we find the so-called Tomb of St. James. An inscription identifies this as the burial place of a family of priests in the second century B.C.; nonetheless, tradition holds this to be the place where St. James took refuge and was later buried. Here again, the attribution is complex and obscure, since it is equally common opinion that this tomb was used by this Apostle as a hermitage during the period between Christ's Crucifixion and His Resurrection. Later, St. James supposedly travelled to the Iberian peninsula, where he evangelized extensively, before returning to Jerusalem. Back in Jerusalem, St. James suffered cruel persecution at the hands of Herod Agrippa I, who had him put to death; the saint's body was then supposedly transported to Santiago de Compostela, on the northern coast of Spain, where it was paid enormous honors, and St. James eventually became the patron saint of all Spain. The tomb carved out of the rock wall in the Valley of Jehosaphat is a portico tomb; the architrave is supported by two columns without fluting, with Doric capitals; the facade stands about fifteen feet above ground level, and the tomb runs almost fifty feet into the cliff.*

8th April 1839

Tomb of St James. Valley of Jehoshaphat

THE PILLAR OF ABSALOM

Plate 70

Most of the tombs that dot the slopes of the Valley of Jehosaphat are of fairly recent date, but the surprising time-eroded monument that is commonly known as the "Tiara of the Pharaoh," because of the conical shape of its covering, is presumed to date from the period of the Second Temple, and would therefore be two thousand years old.

The magnificent tomb, which is also partially carved out of living rock, is believed to be that of Absalom, the rebellious son of David; according to the Holy Scriptures, since Absalom had no sons to whom he could leave his name and his memory, he had a monument built not far

from Jerusalem, and upon it inscribed his name for posterity. Historical tradition, nonetheless, tells us that Absalom, defeated in battle by his father, fled to the forest of Ephrahim, in the Jordan Valley; there he was caught by the victors, slain, and buried in a simple ditch. As so often happens, here too it is difficult to distinguish fact from legend. In any case, the Tomb of Absalom - its lower section extremely reminiscent of the Tomb of Zechariah - remains a magnificent example of Hellenistic architecture. It appears as a cube roughly twenty feet on each face, entirely detached from the sloping limestone ridge of the hill. The faces of the cube are punctuated by half-columns with Ionic capitals and composite corner pillars.

alomys Pillar.
Valley of Jehoshaphat.

The architrave, with carved Doric triglyphs and metopes, supports a parallelipiped element, upon which a low cylinder stands, terminating in a crown with relief decorations; all of this is completed by an odd bell-shaped roof, tall and tapering. The interior of the construction consists of a small burial chamber. David Roberts, who spent the entire afternoon of the 8th of April visiting the Valley of Jehosaphat, was struck by the remarkable similarities between these cliff tombs and the architecture of Petra - in particular, the habit of merging half-columns and corner pilasters seemed identical to him.

8th April 1839

THE FOUNTAIN OF SILOAM

Plate 71

8th April 1839

*A*round the year 1000 B.C., King David conquered Jerusalem and made it his capital; later David's son Solomon built his temple on the hill overlooking the Valley of the Kidron. This choice of location - which so greatly influenced the later development of the city's layout, and which has recently been documented by archeological finds on the slopes to the south of the Mosque of El Aksa - was probably determined by the presence of a spring, back then the only source of fresh water in the entire region.

The Gihon Fountain, also known as the Siloam Fountain, tumbles forth from a deep cleft in the rock in the higher section of the Valley of Jehosaphat. Today one can still reach the spring only by descending a steep stairway carved into the living rock. The spring lies outside the walls and this was the reason why the Jebusites dug an underground tunnel to conduct the fresh water into the city to the Siloam Pool. It was through this narrow passage that the Jews, led by the young David, made their way into Jerusalem, taking the defenders by surprise. The waters of the Siloam Fountain were used as a votive offering by the priests of the temple during the Feast of the Tabernacles. David Roberts toured the entire Valley of Jehosaphat on the afternoon of the 8th of April; while there he carefully sketched the rock-cut tombs of the valley. Although this plate and the two subsequent plates are not dated, it is fair to suppose that they were all completed on that same day, considering the proximity of the three sites and the burial ground.

Fountain of Siloam
Valley of Jehoshaphat.

THE POOL OF SILOAM

Plate 72

Since the spring of Siloam bubbled forth at the back of a cave in the Valley of Jehosaphat, outside the city walls and therefore eminently vulnerable to attack, the inhabitants of Jerusalem were afraid of remaining cut off from

water during a siege. Three centuries after the reign of David, when the threat of an attack by the Assyrians began to loom large, King Hezekiah gave the order to dig a new tunnel, in order to channel the spring waters into the city, to what has since come to be called the Pool of Siloam. The spring was thus connected to the new reservoir by a channel some one thousand seven hundred and fifty feet in length. The stream crossed the hill of Ophel and gushed forth in the Tyropoeon Valley.
An inscription commemorated the completion of the colossal undertaking, which took place in 701 B.C. When the plaque with the inscription was uncovered in 1880, under Ottoman rule, it was transported to Istanbul, where it is still part of the collection of the Museum of Ancient Orient. The English archeologist Charles Warren, in order to study this remarkable piece of hydraulic engineering, made his

way along the entire length of the tunnel on his hands and knees, jotting down a plan of its course as he went. The fruit of his daring labors is displayed in the Archeological Museum of Jerusalem. The Pool of Siloam appears today as a basin of crystal-clear water, located at the mouth of the tunnel, at the end of a trench bounded by stone walls, which can be reached by a stairway.

A popular legend has it that the Virgin Mary came to wash the clothes of the Infant Jesus in this very fountain, and that the Savior used the same water years later in order to restore the sight of a blind man.

8 April 1839

THE FOUNTAIN
OF JOB

Plate 73

8th April 1839

Fountain of Job. Valley of Hinno...

The so-called Fountain of Job is, in reality, an ancient well located just below the point in which the Valley of Jehosaphat joins the valley of Hinnom. It is mentioned in the Book of Joshua and in the Book of Kings, clear signs of an extremely venerable age. Curiously, however, there is no mention of it in any documents dating from the Crusaders' occupation of Jerusalem. One can deduce that the well had long ago fallen into disuse, and that it was restored to operation only following the Arab reconquest. This hypothesis would seem to be supported by the vaguely orientalizing appearance of the structures, as they appear in the drawing and in the description by Roberts. The well, which was roughly one hundred and twenty-five feet in depth, appeared as a large, square basin, fairly irregular, made of massive blocks of stone; one of the sides was occupied by a low building, probably a reservoir, while a taller structure joined it at its corner. Atop this taller structure was a small cupola, and it opened out onto the surface of the water with a spacious acute arch of Islamic style. During the rainy season, the level of the water in the well rose considerably, and the well would even overflow at times. Tradition is divided upon the origin of the name - or even upon the exact name of the fountain. The Christian monks call it the Well of Nehemiah, while the locals called it "Bir Eyub," or the Well of Job. According to the Bible story, this was where the sacred fire of the temple was stored and protected during the Babylonian captivity, until the reconstruction of Jerusalem.

VIEW OF JERUSALEM, LOOKING WESTWARD

Plate 74

9th April 1839

In the panorama of the eastern quarter of the city, we can clearly see the precinct, supported by massive walls, where the mosques of Omar and Al Aksa stand. In this handsome view, it is possible to see how other Islamic constructions of different eras are located around the Dome of the Rock. Among them are the Dome of the Chain, a miniature copy of the Mosque of Omar; Sabeel Qait Bey, a small octagonal structure dating back to the fifteenth century; and the Kadi Burhan el-Din, an elegant outdoor pulpit, for use in the summer. The Mosque of El Aksa, to the left in the illustration, dates from the time of Caliph Walid I, who ordered it built between A.D. 709 and 715, upon the ruins of a Byzantine basilica known as the Church of Purification. It was then destroyed entirely by an earthquake and rebuilt in 1034 in the form that it still largely presents today. Sixty-five years later, during the reign of the Crusaders, it was transformed into a church of the Templar Knights, who called it "Templum Salomonis." When Saladin conquered Jerusalem, El Aksa was turned back into a mosque, which it remains to the present day. Its name means literally "The Most Distant One," because, according to Muslim tradition, it marks the furthest point from Mecca that Mohammed reached during his magical Night Journey to Jerusalem. Right at the foot of the Dome of the Rock and of the Mosque of El Aksa stands the imposing Kotel Maaravi, the Wailing Wall, an enormous wall that once formed a support for the foundations of the Temple of Solomon.

There is no other place on earth so profoundly venerated by the Jewish people. Ever since the times of Roman occupation, followed by the Diaspora, the children of Israel have come here to pray and to show their grief over the destruction of the House of God. Today, this holy place is an open-air synagogue, and Jewish men must come here with their heads covered.

View of Jerusalem, from the South

Plate 75

9th April 1839

The hill that lies to the east of present-day Jerusalem was inhabited from the third millennium B.C. onward by the Canaanites. As early as the second millennium B.C. we find literary documents that mention the city, which was then called Urusalim. When David, upon the death of Saul, decided to gather the various tribes of the Hebrew people into a single kingdom, he chose Jerusalem as his capital due to its advantageous position, girded it with walls, and had his palace built on Mount Zion, where he also moved the Ark of the Covenant. David's son Solomon subsequently enlarged the city, and built the Temple there; this was razed to the ground in 586 B.C., when Nebuchadnezzar conquered the city and took its inhabitants in captivity to Babylon. Upon the return of the Jews from captivity, Jerusalem was rebuilt and enclosed within new walls, but the city never regained its ancient splendor. Conquered in 331 B.C. by Alexander the Great, it then fell under the rule of the Ptolemies, and then the Seleucids, but the resistance of the Maccabees prevented the complete Hellenization of the city. From 63 B.C., Jerusalem fell under the rule of the Romans, and they placed Herod the Great on the throne: during the reign of this king the Temple was rebuilt, and the Fortress Antonia was constructed.

Later on, because of the rapacious greed of the Roman Procurator Gessius Florus, Jerusalem rebelled; besieged first by Vespasian and later by Titus, the city finally fell in A.D. 70. Titus destroyed the city entirely, burnt the Temple, and drove out the inhabitants. Sixty-four years later Hadrian established a Roman colony there called Ælia Capitolina; it was forbidden to Jews. It was not until Constantine became emperor that the city took back its old name. In A.D. 637, the city surrendered to Arabs led by Caliph Omar, who nonetheless granted freedom of worship to both Christians and Jews. This enlightened approach was curtailed under the rule of the Fatimites and the Seljuk Turks, whose harsh behavior helped to spark the Crusades. In 1099 the Holy City was taken by Godfrey of Bouillon, but the Kingdom of Jerusalem endured for less than a century. In 1187, Saladin beat the Latins at the battle of Hattin. Following the short interval of the rule of Frederick II of Swabia, the city remained in Egyptian hands until 1517, the year in which it was conquered by the Turkish Sultan Selim I. Ottoman rule, which continued right up to the First World War, was briefly broken by the occupation of the city by the Egyptian Pasha Ibrahim, between 1831 and 1840, in the very period when Roberts made his tour of the Holy Land.

The Chapel of St. Helena

Plate 76

10th April 1839

Mount Calvary, the site of the crucifixion of Christ, takes its name from the Latin term "calvaria," which means "skull," as do the Hebrew term "Gulgoleth" and the Aramaic word "Gulgoltha." This place name originated from the odd shape of the land here, as well as from a popular superstition that Adam's skull was buried here. Calvary had long been used for public executions, and in the year A.D. 135, it was leveled at the orders of Emperor Hadrian, who had the capitol of his new colony, Aelia Capitolina, built there. Queen Helena came to Jerusalem in the year A.D. 325 on a pilgrimage, in the company of the bishop of Jerusalem, Macarius, guided by a dream in which she was ordered to have excavations made in that precise spot. The excavations quickly unearthed the Holy Sepulchre of Jesus, and - it was even believed - the remains of the True Cross of Christ and of the two thieves. The following year, Helena's son Constantine began construction of a first basilica with five naves, completed in A.D. 335, for the protection of Golgotha and the Holy Sepulchre. Around the Holy Sepulchre, in particular, he ordered the construction of an enormous rotunda topped by a great cupola and called Anastasis, which means "Resurrection."

The entire building was destroyed by the Persians in 614, and rebuilding began fifteen years later, under Abbot Modestus. The new church was severely damaged in 1009 by the armies of the Caliph el-Hakem, and was restored by the Emperor Constantine IX Monomachus. When the Crusaders conquered Jerusalem in July 1099, the entire building was considered to be unworthy to cover the Holy Sepulchre of Christ. The structure was therefore radically renovated, although the same floor plan and the distinctive rotunda were maintained. The new structure was consecrated in 1149; its appearance remained unvaried until 1808, when a terrible fire - possibly arson - seriously damaged the building. When Roberts visited the monument, the restoration had already been completed by the excessively enterprising Greek Orthodox monks. This illustration depicts the intriguing Chapel of St. Helena, a crypt with three naves, supported by four massive columns; a throne is still to be found here, from which the pious queen is said to have overseen the excavation in search of the True Cross. From this room, a narrow staircase leads to another chamber, in which the slab of marble that covered the True Cross of Christ is still kept.

From David Roberts's journal:

10th - After having made four drawings of the Holy Sepulchre, I waited on the new consul, Mr. Young, who arrived here to-day.

Crypt of the Holy Sepulchre

CALVARY

Plate 77

10th April 1839

nfortunately, the reports of the terrible fire that partially destroyed the Holy Sepulchre in 1808 reached Europe at a time when other disasters occupied the public imagination: Rome and the Papal State had just been occupied by Napoleon's troops, and Spain was invaded shortly thereafter. The following year, Pope Pius VII, who had excommunicated the French Emperor, was arrested and imprisoned at Fontainbleau; the cries for help sent out in the wake of the fire by the various congregations of Jerusalem, therefore, fell upon deaf ears in Europe. The Greek Orthodox monks, who had been vying fiercely with the Latin community for centuries over the rights to the church, took canny advantage of the unlooked-to situation.
The Greeks Orthodox monks easily obtained permission to oversee the reconstruction of the basilica, and thereafter became the true adminstrators of the site. Nonetheless, more than a restoration, this was a veritable work of demolition of everything that could be considered to reek of the Latin world. All of the signs of devotion left by armies of pilgrims over the centuries were thus systematically eradicated, such as the inscriptions and the cross that had been carved around the altars; they were replaced by icons and by other typically Greek Orthodox decorations. Among other things, the beautiful sarcophagi of Godfrey of Bouillon, conqueror of Jerusalem, and of his successors, were all destroyed, as was the beautiful edicule that marked the site of the tomb of Christ. Calvary, as it appears in the illustration by Roberts, was covered by a small and ornately decorated chapel. At the center stood an altar, beneath which was a shaft bordered with gilt silver, where the Cross had been placed. On the sides of the altar, two similar holes indicated the points where the crosses of the two thieves had been raised. Currently, Calvary is formed of two adjacent chapels, one of which is Catholic, and the other Greek Orthodox. In the first chapel, two stations of the Way of the Cross show where Jesus was stripped and where He was crucified; in the second chapel, the Twelfth Station marks the point where the Messiah died on the Cross. Behind the altar, three life-sized icons depict Christ on the Cross, the Virgin Mary, and John the Baptist, while between the two chapels stands the small altar of the Stabat Mater.

THE SHRINE OF THE HOLY SEPULCHRE

Plate 78

10th April 1839

*A*t first sight, the interior of the Church of the Holy Sepulchre is almost intimidating with its arcane atmosphere, fraught with the aroma of incense, veiled in dim light, amidst the constant murmuring of the sacred offices. Nonetheless, once the first impression wears off, the church glitters with an incomparable splendor that no one can easily overlook. The plan of the church is the outcome of a series of the most unforeseeable turns of event in history, far more than the product of the intentions of the architects. The quarrels amongst the various religious orders over possession of the Holy Sepulchre did their fair share to increase the level of architectural chaos. Over the centuries, every corner of the building has taken on a specific and precise meaning, and all of the available space around the main structure has been employed in building small chapels that recall events and individuals who played a role in the Crucifixion and the Resurrection of Jesus. The heart of the basilica is, nonetheless, the marble edicule that stands at the center of the Anastasis, or Rotunda, in which the Sepulchre of Christ is still venerated. The small construction, topped by a strangely shaped cupola, owes its fanciful and over-elaborate style to an unknown Greek Orthodox architect who completed it in 1817.

The interior is split up into two small rooms - the first is the Chapel of the Angel, which contains the stone upon which the angel supposedly stood when announcing the Resurrection of Jesus to the pious women, while the second room is the funerary chamber proper, which is also the last station in the Via Dolorosa. The tomb, dug out of the living rock of Golgotha, was donated by Joseph of Arimathea and Nicodemus so that the body of the Messiah could receive adequate burial. Within this narrow space that cannot hold more than six people, an altar bearing an image of the Virgin indicates the corbel-shaped stone, now covered by a slab of finely polished marble, upon which the body of Jesus was laid. Above the Sepulchre hang forty-three silver lamps; thirteen of them belong to the Latin Christians; thirteen belong to the Greek Orthodox; and thirteen belong to the Armenians. The last four belong to the Coptic minority.

Shrine of the Holy Sepulchre
April 14th 1839
David Roberts

THE KATHOLIKON
OF THE HOLY SEPULCHRE

Plate 79

11th April 1839

The central area of the Church of the Holy Sepulchre is formed by the so-called Katholikon, a richly decorated nave, with a rectangular plan and apses, split in two by a tall iconostasis. The iconostasis is a partition or screen upon which icons are placed, separating the sanctuary from the main part of the church; it is a typical feature in Greek Orthodox churches, where the presbytery is always separate, kept out of the sight of the faithful. The iconostasis in question appears as a double row of slender columns. The intercolumnar spaces are blocked by the icons. The nave of the Katholikon is dominated by the "omphalos," a huge cupola from the center of which hangs a majestic lamp. As has been noted elsewhere, following the terrible fire of 1808, the Holy Sepulchre was extensively renovated by the Greek Orthodox monks. With grants from the government of Russia, a country with a special place in its heart for the Eastern Orthodox community in the Holy Land, the Orthodox Greeks became the virtual owners of the church. In this illustration, Roberts is intensely concerned with the exquisite iconostasis and the lavish decorations that encrust the entire interior in a breathtaking, mind-boggling accumulation of wildly different styles. Though the Greek Orthodox forbid any form of sculpture in their churches, what they lack in statues they amply make up for with the profusion of paintings, gilt stuccoes, votive lamps, and fine marble objects. At the center of the nave, below the large lamp, stands a small votive vase with an odd shape, the object of great devotion on the part of all the Christian pilgrims that come here. They believe that the vase in question stands precisely upon the fulcrum, or "belly button," of the world.

The Katholikon as it appears today has varied from the illustration by Roberts; an enormous restoration project has recently restored the church to what is believed to be its original form, dating from the Crusades.

THE POOL OF BETHESDA

Plate 80

12th April 1839

In Latin, the word for pool - "piscina" - was used generically, to describe any basin of water not roofed over, whether that water was used to keep fish or for humans to swim in. In ancient Jerusalem, the great reservoir of fresh water located at the northeast corner of the walls of the temple, not far from the Church of St. Anne, was called "piscina probatica." It must have been a common urge with the earliest Christian monks to give names taken from the Holy Scriptures to just about any important landmark in the City of David; perhaps while the waterproof lining was made during the Roman period. Nearby, during the Byzantine Era, a large church was built, and later the Crusaders built a chapel there. Unfortunately, all of these subsequent constructions, a veritable microcosm of the complex urban history of Jerusalem, were destroyed over the course of the centuries, and today only a few scattered traces remain.

Tradition has it that in the Pool of Bethesda lambs were washed before being sacrificed in the Temple, and the Gospel according to St. John mentions

that urge led them to dub this impressive structure - about three hundred sixty feet in length, some one hundred and thirty feet in width, and about seventy-five feet deep - with the name of Bethesda. The deepest parts of the reservoir date from the era of the Hasmoneans, that Jesus cured the crippled man here. In the illustration by Roberts, the deep trench appears to be choked with rubble and dirt, and small trees even grew on this pile of detritus. Only a part of the basin contained even a puddle of stagnant water, remaining from the spring rains.

From David Roberts's journal:

*April 12th - On my return home after
sketching, found that the consul had
called for me. To-day I have wandered
over the hills, but have not been able
to get a good view of the city.*

VIEW OF JERUSALEM, FROM THE NORTH

Plate 81

13th April 1839

During his excursions to the areas surrounding Jerusalem, Roberts had an opportunity to survey the city from a number of different points of view. These views inspired him to draw a number of striking panoramas. This view, in particular, gives us some idea of the exotic allure of the city, which can capture the imagination and spirit of the artist just as well as the ordinary visitor. Rising on the slopes of gentle hills, fragmented geographically and, yet, at the same time, spiritually indivisible, the City of Gold has always been a crossroads between East and West, between worlds and peoples that are radically different one from another. Many consider Jerusalem to be the very center of the Universe. The city has the quality of a timeless symbol. It is a great town of low houses and narrow streets, along which the ancient and the modern live side by side; in much the same way, the most important sacred monuments of the world's three great monotheistic religions are clustered side by side in the limited space available. The natural backdrop for the very history of modern civilization, Jerusalem boasts a veritable mosaic of cultures. This becomes even clearer when one considers the disconcertingly diverse array of ethnic groups that make up the city's population. Jews, Arabs, Muslims, Christians, and Druses coexist in a delicate state of equilibrium, paradoxically made more stable by their ability to maintain their distinct identities. Perhaps it is in this alchemical equilibrium that we can find the secret of a city that has witnessed bloody internecine battles over millennia, that has been dismembered by political and religious fanatics, but which has always succeeded in reaffirming its sacred and universal standing.

THE GATE OF DAMASCUS

Plate 82

14th–15th April 1839

One of the most remarkable works of architecture in Jerusalem is certainly represented by the city walls, which run some two and a half miles, in part around the perimeter of the original Roman fortifications, and in part around those built during the Crusades. Built with fairly small blocks and recycled materials, the walls - which still enclose the old part of the city - were erected between 1536 and 1542 at the orders of Suleiman the Magnificent when Palestine was under Turkish rule.

The walls, which still possess the original battlements, communication trenches, and interior stairways, are punctuated by the eight gates, seven of which, massive and well proportioned, were built upon the foundations of older gates; a number of elements of these gates have also been incorporated. When David Roberts visited Jerusalem, only four gates, corresponding to the four cardinal points, were open. Of the eight gates, the most handsome and best known is the Damascus Gate, once known as Bal-el-Amud. The gate takes its modern name from the fact that

it leads to the road for Syria and the north. Built astride an ogival arch set between two imposing square towers with corner sentry-turrets, this gate is somewhat more ornate than the other seven. Today, just as when Roberts, disguised as an Arab with a train of camels and an entourage of servants, drew it, a marketplace stood nearby, with the noise of haggling and the aroma of spices wafting over all. In the nearby money-changing bureaus, one might almost expect to see the glitter of gold and silver coins on the pans of finely wrought balances; nonetheless, even though over time the precious metals have been replaced by folding bills and calculators, the mercantile tradition of the place has remained solidly anchored, seemingly deep in the stones themselves. This drawing bears the date of the 14th of April - the next day Roberts left Jerusalem and set out for Nablus. The notes written in Roberts's journal for that date inform us that on that night while sleeping in their tents, he and his entourage were alarmed at the clearly encroaching presence of jackals.

FROM JERUSALEM TO BAALBEC

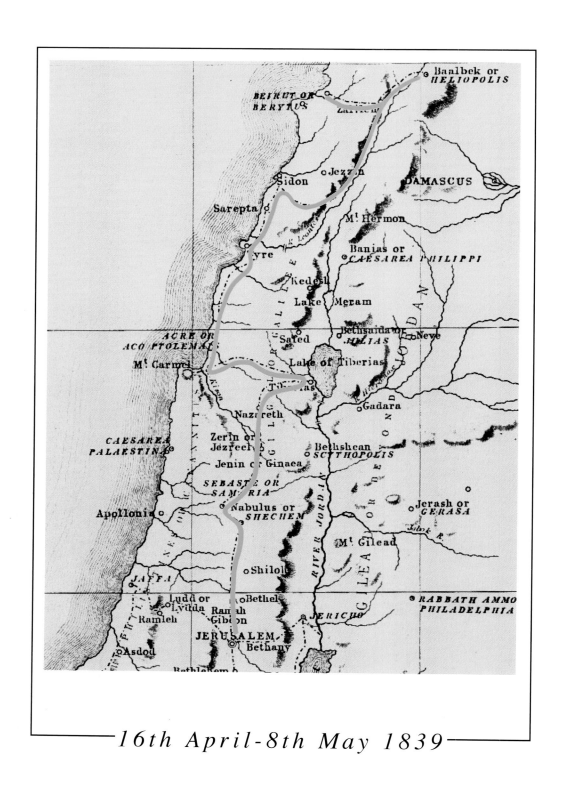

16th April-8th May 1839

The
HOLY LAND

Syria, Idumea, Arabia, Egypt & Nubia.

FROM DRAWINGS MADE ON THE SPOT BY

David Roberts, R.A.

WITH HISTORICAL DESCRIPTIONS BY

THE REV? GEORGE CROLY. L.L.D.

LITHOGRAPHED BY

LOUIS HAGHE.

VOL 2

David Roberts. R.A.

Baalbec, from the Fountain. May 7th 1839.

LONDON. F. G. MOON, 20, THREADNEEDLE STREET.
PUBLISHER IN ORDINARY TO HER MAJESTY.
MDCCCXLIII.

VIEW OF NABLUS

Plate 83

16th April 1839

With typically British precision, David Roberts noted that he entered Nablus around three in the afternoon on the 16th of April. Considering the date that appears on the margin of the drawing, the direction in which the caravan shown here is heading, presumably the same of Roberts himself, and the exact documentation of the journal, we should note that this illustration certainly refers to the trip away from the village, and not to the arrival in the village, as is erroneously noted on the lithograph itself. Nablus, the ancient Shechem mentioned in the Old Testament, lies between Mount Ebal and Mount Gerizim, some thirty miles to the north of Jerusalem, at the mouth of a depression that runs all the way to the Mediterranean Sea. The city, which is today considered to be the chief trading center in all of Samaria and a major agricultural marketplace, was given its name by Titus, who rebuilt it in A.D. 70 and called it Flavia Neapolis, in honor of his father, Titus Flavius Vespasianus, or Vespasian. The valley in which it lies, made particularly fertile by an abundance of springs, appears luxuriant in contrast with the aridity of the surrounding highlands. Even in the distant past, the area was famed for its fruit orchards. It is not surprising that Roberts should have been surprised at the welcoming and orderly appearance of the town, whose inhabitants seemed to him to be among the most prosperous of all those he had seen thus far in Palestine.

From David Roberts's journal:

April 16th - The situation of the town is beautiful. It is placed between the mountains Ebal and Gerizim, and is well sheltered from the north and south winds...

NABLUS, ANCIENT SHECHEM

Plate 84

16th April 1839

The small and bustling town of Nablus, which thrives on farming and small industry, has also preserved intact the synagogue of the Samaritans, as well as the marketplace and lore of the old quarters. Just like the names of Hebron, Jericho, and other Israeli cities, the name of Shechem is familiar to a great many Jews. It was here, in fact, that the Lord promised Abraham that he would rule over the land of Canaan, it was here that the Ark of the Covenant was set down, and it was here - later - that the twelve tribes of Israel assembled to proclaim king the successor of Solomon. The sect of the Samaritans originated at Shechem around the eighth century B.C. Their origin actually dates from the deportation of the Jews from the northern kingdom by the Assyrians, when many Asiatic colonizers arrived in the region and merged with the surviving population. It was then that the Jews, returning from exodus in Babylon, set about rebuilding the Temple and the city of Jerusalem; the Samaritans offered to help but were rudely rebuffed. The Samaritans then built a temple of their own on Mount Garizim, marking their definitive break with the Jews. In 129 B.C., John Hyrcanus destroyed Shechem and the temple; the temple was not rebuilt. The religion is rejected by Orthodox Judaism because of its syncretism and because it does not recognize the authority of the Talmud. Only a few hundred Samaritans survive, living in two separate communities. One is at Holon, not far from Tel Aviv; the other is here in Nablus, and is referred to as Somerin, or "the Guardians," as they consider themselves to be faithful custodians of the Revelation. Each year, at Easter, the Samaritan faithful climb Mount Gerizim, where they celebrate the holiday in the ruins of their ancient temple.

JACOB'S WELL AT NABLUS

Plate 85

*I*n the
*Samaritan synagogue at
Nablus, the famous codex of the
Pentateuch is preserved. The
Pentateuch, the first five books
of the Old Testament, is the only
form of the Sacred Scriptures
recognized by the members of
the sect. Knowledge of this
Pentateuch had reached as early
a writer as St. Jerome, yet the
surviving transcription of the
archaic Hebrew characters dates
back no further than the twelfth
or the eleventh century A.D.
David Roberts noted in his
journal that he visited the
synagogue on the 17th of April
and, slightly later, that he went*

*to see the so-called Well of Jacob,
which lies just south of Nablus
on the road to Jerusalem. With a
sharp note of disappointment, he
wrote that the holy place looked
like nothing more than a heap of
abandoned rubble. There were
only a few fragments of columns,
partly buried but still standing
as mute witnesses to the church
that, according to popular lore,
was built by Queen Helena.*

*With well-reasoned
considerations, Roberts goes on
to show that just as the ruins of
the church are in all likelihood
less ancient than is commonly
believed, the identification of the
well as the one where Jesus met
the Samaritan can be readily
rejected. In the same area, in
fact, there are three or four other
springs that jibe perfectly with
the description found in the*

Gospels. Nonetheless, here too it is wise to give credence to that which has been accepted by generations of the faithful as true, as their centuries of devotion and continuing adoration confer a certain historical dignity to the few concrete bits of evidence that survive.

From David Roberts's journal:

April 17th - I visited the synagogue of the ancient Samaritans, and was shown there two very ancient MSS. of the Pentateuch. Went to the Well of Jacob, where the interview took place between our Saviour and the woman of Samaria.

17th April 1839

Tomb of Joseph at Shechem.

THE TOMB OF JOSEPH AT NABLUS

Plate 86

17th April 1839

Near Nablus, in a village called Askar, is a tomb in which tradition holds that Joseph and his two sons, Ephraim and Manasseh, heads of the two tribes of Israel that bore their names, were buried. The special holiness of this place, which has never waned over the centuries, is due to the undying reverence paid to the figure of Joseph. A man who was more pious and just than any other, Joseph died in the land of Egypt in the certain belief that Palestine was the land promised to his people. When, during the Exodus, the Jews brought the body of Joseph with them, Jacob purchased, for one hundred pieces of silver, the land in which to bury him, quite close to the ancient town of Shechem, now known as Nablus. This event supposedly sanctioned in formal terms the right of the Jewish people to the land of Canaan.

In this illustration by David Roberts, who came here shortly after visiting Jacob's Well, Joseph's Tomb appears as a massive block that has been plastered over: low and squat. On one side, a shallow niche has been carved, where a number of small lamps burn, probably brought as marks of devotion by one of the faithful. The two blocks of roughly squared stone that stand on either side of the tomb are traditionally considered to be the headstones of Ephraim and Manasseh.

SEBASTE, ANCIENT SAMARIA

Plate 87

*A*fter leaving Nablus on the afternoon of the 17th, David Roberts and his travelling companions rode for two and a half hours before they sighted the ancient Samaria, now known as Sebaste. The city was founded in 925 B.C. by King Omri of Israel; it became the third capital of the kingdom, after Shechem and Tirza. Samaria was attacked repeatedly by the Arameans, Assyrians, and then Persians; it was destroyed by Alexander the Great, and then again by John Hyrcanus, and was subsequently rebuilt by Herod the Great, who named it Sebaste (i.e., Augusta, in honor of Octavian Augustus). Herod then handed the city over to the Romans.

The modern town stands on the eastern part of the hill, while the peak of the hill is occupied by an intriguing archeological zone, that was explored by American archeology teams as early as the first few decades of this century. It is possible to admire the remains of the palace of King Omri as well as the ruins of a truly splendid Roman forum, and - above all - the Church of St. John the Baptist built by the Crusaders on the foundations of a previously existing Byzantine temple. In the crypt of this church, the relics of John the Baptist and the prophets Elisha and Elijah were venerated. In his diary, Roberts noted that the valley of Sebaste, so luxuriant and tranquil, might easily have passed for a stretch of English countryside, in stark contrast with the arid desolation found in the area around Jerusalem. With a typically Romantic sensibility, the artist described the emotions that surged up in him at the sight of the ruins of Sebaste, so silent and deserted, bathed in the warm light of sunset. In the drawing, one can clearly see the impressive colonnade of the palace of Herod, which originally had the extent of three thousand feet; the function that this colonnade intended to serve is still the object of considerable speculation. Following a period of great splendor, Sebaste underwent a rapid decline in inverse proportion to the rise of nearby Nablus; by the Middle Ages, the city already lay in ruins.

castra antiqua. Samaria. April 17th 1839.

17th April 1839

RUINS OF THE CHURCH OF ST. JOHN THE BAPTIST AT SEBASTE

Plate 88

18th April 1839

*R*oberts, who had ordered the tents pitched right at the foot of the hill upon which stand the ruins of Sebaste, toured the entire area on the 17th and 18th of April, and drew up a careful description. The remains of the walls of the Church of St. John the Baptist, which was built on the site of the martyrdom and decapitation of the saint, still stood to a considerable height, and the high, narrow windows presented decorations in the Norman style. Grotesque naves and the higher windows were more Gothic in style. The columns had the proportions of the Corinthian order; the material used in the construction of the church was chiefly the tufa quarried in the surrounding hills. At the center of the nave, which was just almost one hundred and fifty feet in length, lay the tomb of a sheik. In addition to his architectural observations, Roberts noted that, though popular tradition might hold that Queen Helena was

figures and anthropomorphic heads adorned the many stone blocks that were scattered here and there. The apse and the altar showed clear signs of Greek Orthodox influence, as did the lower windows in the apse, while the acute arches of the responsible for the foundation of the church, the monument itself could more rightly be attributed to the Crusading Knights of St. John; the numerous crosses carved into the rock as tokens of devotion seem to support this hypothesis.

Ruins of The Church of St. John. Sabaste

From David Roberts's journal:

April 18th - In the middle of the city (if a few wretched hovels deserve such a name), rising over vast arches of hewn stone, are the ruins of a Christian church, the architecture of which must have been very perfect...

JENIN, ANCIENT JEZREEL

Plate 89

19th April 1839

From Roberts's journal, we learn that the artist's caravan left the ruins of Sebaste on the afternoon of the 18th of April, and that it was late at night by the time the caravan reached the village of Abate, which is set on the peak of a hill not far from a lake. There Roberts and his fellow travellers finally pitched their tents. The male population of the village was mostly made up of the elderly and the infirm, since most of the young men had been conscripted into the army. Roberts was especially impressed with the clothing worn by the women of the place, of which he gives us a brief but thorough description.

"The dress consists of a loose white robe, and a red sash; a red handkerchief is bound round the head; a scarf of the same colour covering the under part of the face, falls down over the back, and a string of large silver coins hangs dangling from the dark hair."

The group of travellers set out at dawn, and was quickly within sight of Jenin, a pleasant village set at the mouth of a valley that opens out onto the fertile plain of Esdraelon. Set in a luxuriant oasis, the town is now a prosperous farming center, capital of the district with the same name.

It is believed that the town occupies the site of the ancient Jezreel, but not all of the scholars are in agreement on this. The only certain information that we have is that Jenin was first mentioned around the time of the Crusades, and that its name became increasingly familiar to the pilgrims who came to Palestine. This was a result of its favorable position on the road that leads to Nazareth from Jerusalem. Roberts sketched the town, surrounded by palm groves, alongside a pleasant stream, as if to emphasize the fertility of the region.

MOUNT TABOR

Plate 90

19th April 1839

After passing through Jenin, Roberts and his travelling companions followed a track that was to take them to Nazareth, after skirting the plain of Esdraelon. Mentioned several times in the Bible, the fertile plain of Esdraelon, crossed by the Kishon River, opens out amidst the hills of northern Samaria and between Carmel to the south and Galilee to the north. Crisscrossed by ancient and important roads and routes, this plain was the site of famous battles: Barak conquered the Medianites; Ahab routed the Syrians; Saul was conquered and killed by the Philistines; Josiah was beaten by the pharaoh Necho. The land was reclaimed and improved centuries ago and today is an extremely populous and productive farm land. The highlands that overlook it are Gilboa, Hermon, and the very imposing Mount Tabor, certainly the geographic feature that most captured the imagination of David Roberts. He sketched the mountain although he did note that he found it far less grand than he had gathered from the drawings he had seen of it by others. Although the mountain is handsome and well proportioned, it long ago lost its daunting austerity because of the ongoing process of settlement and reclamation that local farmers have been carrying forward over the years, shaping the slopes and smoothing away the mountain's most jagged edges. On the other hand, Roberts concluded in his notes that this was the same fate that befell practically every mountain and hill in Palestine, where farming softens everything. The caravan shown in the foreground in the drawing was a group of Christian pilgrims returning to Jerusalem from Damascus. Roberts came upon the caravan as the pilgrims were taking their noonday rest.

NAZARETH

Plate 91

19th April 1839

The journal notes that the trail leading to Nazareth at first wound steeply among the hills, and then descended without warning to the tiny village, which almost seemed to burrow and nestle into the protective embrace of the hills. In both Arabic and Hebrew, the name Nazareth means "The Guardian," and while this may have originally been a reference to the strategic location of the village - which overlooks the plain of Esdrelon - today it seems to have more to do with the role that history has reserved for it, of being the guardian of Christian tradition, under the watchful administration of the Franciscan brothers. Although Nazareth has been inhabited from time out of mind, the town in which Jesus was grown up has only become a full-fledged town in recent years.

The old houses with their white-plaster coats reach almost to the peak of the hill where the Church of Jesus the Adolescent now stands, while further down modern buildings stand in neat rows. The fairly heterogeneous makeup of the urban structure corresponds to an equally complex makeup in ethnic and religious terms. While the Muslims live in the old town and the Jews live in the new quarter of Illit, there are a number of other communities, such as Catholics, Greek Orthodox, Maronites, and others belonging to minor creeds. Each of these groups now possesses its own churches and other institutions. When Roberts visited here, and was greeted by the Father Superior of the Latin convent, the population of Nazareth was just three thousand.

THE CHURCH OF THE ANNUNCIATION

Plate 92

Nazareth was inhabited exclusively by Jews until the fourth century A.D. Since the Holy Scriptures state that the birth of Jesus was announced to Mary in this precise village, the earliest Christians took up residence here and began to build a church of their own. This church was in time replaced by a Byzantine basilica, and then by a church built by Crusaders - only a few fragments survive of both of these structures. Long after Saladin won the town back to Arab rule in 1187, St. Louis, King of France came and visited Nazareth in 1252. In 1363, the Mameluke sultan Baibars had all of the Christian sacred buildings in the town destroyed,

and for more than four centuries, the place was little more than an expanse of ruins. In 1620, the Franciscans built a church and a convent here, expanding them in 1730; it was around these structures that the modern town grew. The Franciscan church, finally, was knocked down in 1655 to make way for the larger and more impressive project designed by the Italian architect Giovanni Muzio.

The Church of the Annunciation is the largest Christian church in all of the Middle East; it was made possible through a grant from the State of Israel.
The illustration by David Roberts clearly shows us the interior of the church as it appeared in April of 1839.
The structure is articulated over three floors, which are connected by stairways.

The highest level is occupied by
the choir, and is reserved for
monks. The intermediate level
is open to the faithful, and the
lowest level conceals the ruins of
the Cave of the Annunciation.
The monument, which shows
a clear Baroque influence,
is lavishly bestrewn with
decoration - votive images,
candelabra, silver lamps,
exquisite damasks, all cover the
pillars and envelop the main altar.

20th April 1839

THE SHRINE OF THE ANNUNCIATION

Plate 93

20th April 1839

*S*ituated beneath the Church of the Annunciation was a small subterranean chamber in which there stood an altar, supposedly marking the exact spot in which the Angel appeared before the Virgin Mary in order to announce the divine mission that awaited her.

The two columns that still stood on either side of the altar when David Roberts made his visit to Nazareth were said to have been the work of the Queen Helena, who supposedly had them erected on the column simply levitated in midair without the slightest structural support, by divine will; nonetheless, to the mind of an unprejudiced observer, it seemed pretty clear that the fragment of column was solidly fastened to the ceiling. In fact, the upper section proved to be made of gray marble, while the lower section was without question a block of Cipolino marble.

All the same, the renown of these two columns amongst the

the site of the Annunciation because she had had a premonitory dream. One of the two columns, clearly visible in this illustration, had been shattered by a Turkish pasha who had come in avid search of hidden treasure; in the wake of such a desecration, it is said, the pasha lost his sight. The monks claimed that the upper section of gullible pilgrims was such that each one of them would rub up against them reverently and with devotion, secure in the knowledge that such contact provided sure balm against all ills and calamities. And on the other hand, the reasoning of faith often sorely twists and mishandles the reasoning of logic, producing what could only be called superstition; the most innocent-minded of superstitions, but superstition nonetheless.

And so tradition had it that it was precisely in the Grotto that the Virgin Mary spent a considerable portion of her youth, and above this tiny chamber stood the Holy House, which the Angels first

transported to Dalmatia, and then to a woods near Recanati, and finally to Loreto - all to preserve it from profanation by the Muslims. It should further be noted that the earliest author to identify the small sanctuary of Loreto as the "House of Nazareth" was Pietro di Giorgio Tolomei da Teramo, who wrote an account in 1472 that was soon after expanded upon by Gerolamo Angelita, winning enormous and widespread credence in the popular imagination; further, the popes that found themselves in the situation of conferring privileges to the Sanctuary - Julius II and Leo X - considered it little more than a pious belief.

Convent of the Terra Santa Nazareth. April 21st 1839.

David Roberts

THE CONVENT OF THE TERRA SANTA, NAZARETH

Plate 94

20th April 1839

The town of Nazareth lies in an enchanting amphitheater of hills, embellished by olive groves, fig trees, almond trees, and cypresses; it occupies a strategic location that nearly all of the invaders of the Holy Land over the millennia have tried to occupy securely. Aside from the Church of the Annunciation, Nazareth boasts a number of other places that are holy to Christians, such as the Fountain of the Virgin, or what is commonly said to be the Workshop of Joseph, which forms part of the Franciscan Monastery of the Terra Santa. Just a mile out of town, moreover, stands the rock which has been venerated since ancient times as the site of the dramatic effort to throw Jesus down after his sermon in the Synagogue, as narrated by St. Luke. At the foot of the rock stands a small Maronite Christian church.

In this illustration by Roberts, Nazareth appears as a tiny cluster of houses, dominated by the minaret of a mosque, and by the bulk of the Franciscan convent; the latter, built around 1632 on the foundations of an earlier church, and then partially fortified a century later, had just been restored and enjoyed a certain wealth. Nowadays, Nazareth is a sort of Christian enclave within the borders of Galilee, with a sizable Arab population. Galilee has always been a transit spot, vulnerable to invaders, but especially a place of miracles. Only during the past few years has Galilee been rescued from the decline and neglect into which it had fallen and rescued from the encroaching elements. If it has become the garden spot of Israel today, that is to the everlasting credit of the hard-working and caring Hebrew pioneers.

THE FOUNTAIN OF THE VIRGIN

Plate 95

20th April 1839

The so-called *Fountain of the Virgin, the only source of drinkable water in the area around Nazareth, was held in great respect by Christian pilgrims, because tradition held that Mary went out to draw water from it every day, during her youth. The fountain spills forth beneath the Greek Orthodox Church of the Assumption, set in a small niche beneath an arch, at the very spot where the Virgin is said to have been greeted and hailed by the Archangel*

Gabriel. The basin was made out of what appeared to have originally been a sarcophagus. The spring itself, with a fairly feeble flow of water, lies at a certain distance, and the waters are conveyed to the fountain through a rough stone channel. During the summer, the source would dry up from time to time, and the inhabitants of Nazareth were then forced to go to other villages for their fresh water

needs. The women shown in this illustration constitute an interesting documentation of the women's clothing during the first half of the nineteenth century; among other things, Roberts noted that many of them wore long bangles or chains made up of gold and silver coins, which hung on either side of their faces, forming a magnificent contrast with their long black tresses, and that the younger girls in particular were extremely lovely in appearance. Oddly enough,

although they realized that they were in the presence of a Christian, they made absolutely no effort to cover their faces. The dating of this illustration, like that of plates 91 and 94, should certainly be modified, according to what is stated in the painter's journal; here, Roberts clearly states that he was in Nazareth between the 19th and the 20th of April 1839.

Fountain of the Virgin, Nazareth. April 21st 1839.

From David Roberts's journal:

April 20th - Made two coloured drawings of the chapel, one of the Grotto or Chapel of the Annunciation, and two views of the town. Several objects of interest are pointed out to the pilgrim: the workshop of Joseph, the stone on which Christ sat with his disciples, and the fountain to which the Virgin went for water.

CANA OF GALILEE

Plate 96

21st April 1839

*R*oberts left Nazareth on the morning of the 21st of April, and reached Cana in Galilee around midday, after a pleasant canter that lasted a little longer than an hour. The village was formed by forty or fifty little huts, some of which were in ruins, and while its appearance might be unassuming if not actually squalid, the whole inspired him with an irrepressible sense of the holy. In Cana, in fact - according to the Gospels - Jesus performed His first miracle, changing water into wine at a wedding banquet, and, shortly thereafter, healing the son of the wealthiest man in the town who came to greet him - this upon his return from Judea. The priest of the little Greek Orthodox church that stood at the foot of the hill - and which was believed to have been built upon the remains of the home in which the miracle supposedly happened - showed Roberts a priceless relic - this, the priest said, was one of the jars in which Christ had transformed the water into wine. Not far from the church, a building lay in ruins, and it was generally indicated as the home in which Christ had lived as a guest for a certain period of time. Despite the descriptions offered by the Gospel and accepted in popular devotion, the exact location of the town of Cana is a matter of some controversy, and the current site is said to be variously Kefr Kenna, which is near Nazareth, and Kefr Qana, only a little distance off. Roberts remained in the village for only a few hours, and then continued his voyage, heading for the Sea of Galilee.

THE FOUNTAIN OF CANA

Plate 97

Fountain at Cana, April 21st 1839.

The fountain shown in this illustration is believed to be the one from which Jesus is said to have drawn the water that he used in performing his first miracle; Roberts noted that the water was plentiful and remarkably pure, and that there were no other sources of fresh water for many miles around. And this fact would seem to reinforce the attribution, which was generally accepted. The large basin made of marble decorated with friezes that stood not far from the fountain was in fact a Roman sarcophagus, long since given over to use as a drinking trough for the domestic beasts, in accordance with a custom that had become fairly widespread in Palestine and in the entire Mediterranean basin. The women of Cana would go to the fountain every day, bearing jars made of the same materials, and the same size and shape as those described in the Bible. And the Christian pilgrims would often stay awhile around the fountain, quenching their thirst and participating in what almost seemed a sacred ceremony prior to entering the village. In ancient times, the miracle of the wedding banquet of Cana was depicted in the frescoes in the catacombs of Domitilla in Rome, in the mosaics of the Baptistery in Naples, and in those found in the Basilica of St. Apollinare Nuovo in Ravenna.

Afterwards, the "Wedding at Cana" was painted by Giotto in the Chapel of the Scrovegni, in Padua. During the Renaissance and the two centuries that followed it, it became a fairly common subject, used by Gérard David, by Longhi, and by Tintoretto, among others. The best known painting of the Wedding at Cana is certainly the one painted by Paolo Veronese, now at the Louvre, in which many famous personalities of the era appear as guests at the wedding banquet: Francis I, Charles V, Queen Mary I of England, better known as Bloody Mary, Suleiman the Magnificent, Titian, and Paolo Veronese himself, along with his brother.

From David Roberts's journal:

21st, Sunday - ...There is a small Greek church, said to cover the place formerly occupied by the house in which the marriage took place.
A ruined House is pointed out as the residence of our Saviour, and on entering the village we were shown a fountain from whence the water was said to have been taken.

21st April 1839

226

THE SEA OF GALILEE

Plate 98

21st April 1839

After leaving the village of Cana behind him and riding for about five hours through a pleasant landscape, Roberts finally came within sight of the Sea of Tiberias, a placid body of water upon whose enameled waters not a single vessel could be seen. From high atop the hill, at the foot of which stood the ruins of the ancient city of Tiberias - destroyed just a few years before by a terrible earthquake - the gaze of the English artist surveyed a panorama that was enchanting and at the same time majestic. Truly the jewel of Galilee, brilliant as an emerald, the Sea of Tiberias lies burrowed about six hundred fifty feet below sea level, held tight by a wreath of mountain peaks adorned with luxuriant vegetation. The lake receives the waters of the Jordan River, which rises at the foot of Mount Hermon and then runs down to the depression of the Dead Sea; one distinctive feature of this lake is its brackish water, populated by a great variety of fish. The shores of the lake were the setting for the preaching of Jesus, and the group of Apostles came into existence here.

According to the traditional interpretation of the Gospels, the miracle of the loaves and fish took place at Tabgha, while not far off is the home of St. Peter's home of Kapharnaon, as well as the Mount of the Beatitudes, where Jesus appeared before the Apostles. The ancient power that imbues the Sea of Galilee has long held sway over the imagination. Indeed, two thousand years ago the Jew historian Flavius Josephus, who wrote in Latin, was full of admiration in his description of the landscape surrounding the lake.

From David Roberts's journal:

April 21st, Sunday - Passing on through a beautiful country... we came in sight of the Sea of Galilee. Far to the left is Mount Hermon, and near to us is Safed, where the Jews expect the Messiah to reign forty years before entering Jerusalem...

THE LAKE OF TIBERIAS, VIEW TOWARDS MOUNT HERMON

Plate 99

21st April 1839

The Lake of Tiberias, also known as the Lake of Gennesareth or the Lake of Kinneret, is a small inland sea that formed toward the end of the Tertiary Period following the same tectonic depression that affected the Jordan Valley and led to the creation of the Dead Sea. The Dead Sea formed as a result of the interruption of the flow of the Jordan toward the Gulf of Aqaba. Over the millennia, the total aridity and high average temperature of the region, in combination with the shallowness and the greater surface area of the Dead Sea in comparison with the Sea of Tiberias, created a situation in which the evaporation was equal to and in some cases superior to the flow of the Jordan, so that the waters of the Dead Sea are constantly increasing in salinity and at the same time declining in volume. Regularly fed by the waters of the Jordan, which freshen the water somewhat, the Lake of Tiberias attains a depth of one hundred and sixty feet and constitutes a valuable reserve for the entire region. The remarkable location makes it subject to frequent winter tempests, an observation that is also made in the Gospels, while in the summer the surface is incessantly ruffled by a pleasant breeze. Because the water so abounds in fish, thousands of aquatic birds line the shores and the stands of reeds of this tiny "sea" just fourteen and a half miles long, with water so transparent that Roberts was dumbfounded. The artist spent much of the day at Tiberias on the 22nd of April, taking the time to tour the city and the surrounding countryside, making a few thoroughgoing sketches as he went. In this plate, Mount Hermon appears on the horizon in all its majesty, while at the foot of the hill lie the remains of the ancient town.

Town of Tiberias, looking towards Lebanon.

David Roberts. R.A.

TIBERIAS, LOOKING TOWARD LEBANON

Plate 100

21st April 1839

Tiberias was a Roman city famous for its curative hot springs. Today, it has become a winter spa and a well equipped tourist attraction. The city is also well known outside the narrow boundaries of Israel. It was founded in 26 B.C. by Herod Antipas, tetrarch of Galilee, the son of Herod the Great. The city's name was clearly intended to honor the emperor Tiberius. There are those, however, who attribute the name Tiberias to the Hebrew term "tabur," which means belly-button, since the lake that bears the same name has something like the shape of a belly-button. Following the destruction of the Temple of Jerusalem, a major rabbinical school was founded here. It was at that school that great scholars developed the phonetics of Hebrew writing. During the reign of Constantine, Tiberias was an episcopal see, but the city was conquered by the Arabs in A.D. 637. It then became the capital of the province of Jordan. During the First Crusade, Tiberias was occupied by the Christians and was ceded as part of the feud of Tancred. In 1187, however, it was returned to Arab rule, and four centuries later it fell under the sway of the Turks, who held the city until World War I. Each of these various occupying nations left marks of their rule in the urban fabric of the city. Two of the most intriguing monuments, however, are certainly the tomb of the Rabbi Meir Ba'al Haness and the tomb of the rabbi and martyr Akiva, both of which are sacred destinations for Jewish pilgrims. This view of the city and the lake, set beneath the snowy peaks of the mountains of Lebanon, may be visually striking, but it is also quite important in historical terms. Roberts, in fact, believed that the ruins that can be seen in the foreground were the remains of the ancient baths of Tiberias. This hypothesis is supported by the presence of numerous hot springs in the immediate vicinity. In Hebrew, these springs are called Hame Tverla, and they are said to have astonishing qualities for the treatment of rheumatism.

From David Roberts's journal:

21st April, Sunday - To the south the Jordan flows from the lake to the Dead Sea, and close to the lake lies the ancient town of Tiberias, which, with 400 of its inhabitants, was destroyed by an earthquake some years since... the ruins of a small mosque stand near the entrance to the town, and we passed to-day the foundations of more than one ancient city with excavations in the rocks.

TIBERIAS, SEEN FROM THE WALLS

Plate 101

Tiberias was largely laid waste by an earthquake in January 1837, and when Roberts visited the place it still was nothing more than an expanse of ruins, amidst which the population wandered in shock, battered by tragedy. Few buildings had survived the disaster, and the remains of a mosque were visible at the entrance to the town. Here and there amidst the rubble a few huts stood, where a number of elderly Jews lived, who had come there to spend the last days of their lives, through the generosity of their brethren scattered throughout the world. Tiberias is in fact one of the four holy cities of Judea, along with Jerusalem, Hebron, and Safed. The last named city appears in the distance in the illustration, with the mountains of Lebanon in the distance. This city, which is believed to be the site of the ancient Bethulia, became one of the greatest centers for the study of the Talmud and for Talmudic culture after the Jews were expelled from Spain, in 1492. The exiles, after founding a major rabbinical school, set up the first printing press in Israel in 1563. In Safed, great men of learning found refuge, such as Moshe Cordovero, Isaac Louria, Israel Najara, and a great many others, who devoted themselves to the study of the Holy Scriptures, developing an approach to exegesis that brought them to an understanding of the Cabala, a term used to describe a mystical Jewish system of interpretation of the Scriptures, based on the belief that every word, letter, number, and even accent of the Scriptures contains mysteries. Roberts left the Sea of Tiberias on the afternoon of the 22nd of April, headed for the coast, and spent the night camped near the only fountain that exists in the area.

David Roberts R.A.

From David Roberts's journal:

April 22nd - To-day I made few sketches of the town, or rather of its remains - for every part has been more or less destroyed by earthquakes. The city wall, which is Saracenic, has been built of large square stones, now thrown down and rent from top to bottom...

22nd April 1839

St. Jean d'Acre. April 23rd 1839

ST. JEAN D'ACRE,
SEEN FROM THE SEA

Plate 102

23rd April 1839

Extending along the furthest tip of land at the mouth of Haifa Bay Akko, or Acre, is one of the oldest cities in the world: silent, brooding, and enclosed by walls built by the Crusaders, it seems to be watching over the eternal vastness of the Mediterranean. Today it is Israel's most important harbor. For centuries it was coveted by invaders and interlopers for its strategic location on the gulf that bears its name. Founded in the remote eras of antiquity, Akko has been ruled by Egyptians, Assyrians, Persians, and Romans. Invaded by the Arabs in A.D. 638, it was besieged by Richard the Lion-Hearted and taken from Saladin in 1191, becoming the capital of the Crusaders' Kingdom. Its European name, St. Jean d'Acre, derives from the Hospitaler Brothers of St. John, better known as the Knights of St. John, who made it their capital. In 1291, the Muslims returned and the city quickly fell into disrepair and ruin. It was not until the eighteenth century that the Turkish emirs restored the city. and in 1799, stoutly resisted a lengthy siege laid by Napoleon; the British fleet had assisted the besieged city. Roberts reached the city during the early hours of the afternoon of the 23rd and was immediately impressed by the grandeur of the place. A large warship lay at anchor in the harbor, while the city's fortifications towered over the plain in sharp contrast with the blue of the sea, forming a panorama that, in Roberts's own words, would have satisfied the esthetic sense of Turner himself. Roberts ordered the tents pitched near the city walls and set out to wander the streets of the city where he soon realized that many of the buildings still bore evident scars from the recent war.

This lithograph by Roberts emphasizes the odd Ottoman architectural style of the city, chiefly the result of the urban planning and renovation carried out by Ahmed el Jazzar, the seventeenth-century pasha who was responsible for the construction of the mosque that bears his name, the largest in all Israel. Built in 1781, it is still a major spiritual center for the Muslim community in Israel.

From David Roberts's journal:

April 23rd - Left at half-past 8 for St. Jean d'Acre, which we came in sight of at 3 o'clock. The situation is striking - a promontory to the north of the bay, Mount Carmel rising on the south...

ST. JEAN D'ACRE,
SEEN FROM THE LAND

Plate 103

23rd April 1839

The ancient stones of Akko, erected over the centuries of a history that has been stormy and often bloody - the Palace of the Knights, the subterranean crypt of the Crusaders, the Arabic caravansaries - speak eloquently of merchants and warriors, of sieges beyond count, of vast destruction followed by rebirth, and of tireless, incessant toil. In the past, among the trades plied in Akko there was the extraction and the application of purple dye, as well as the manufacture of glass. In this connection, we should note that the Roman historian Pliny considered that the city deserved credit for the invention of the techniques vital to the production of glass. Known in Roman times as Colonia Claudia Felix, the adjective "Felix," meaning happy or blessed, was a term that clearly referred to opulence or prosperity. Mentioned often in the Bible and in the papyri of the Pharaohs of Ancient Egypt, Akko had always been a center of crucial importance to the economic prosperity of the entire region; although the city faced some extremely dire moments, it always survived with great aplomb. Roberts arrived in Akko during an extremely serious military and political crisis, and the plate we reproduce here bears witness to the military history of the period. The troops of the pasha of Egypt had taken the city in 1832, badly trouncing the Turkish army; seven years later, the same Turkish army invaded Syria, but was once again defeated at Nizip, once again frustrated in the attempt to reach the bay of Akko. The city, therefore, was held by a sizable Egyptian garrison; Roberts here portrays the garrison as it conducted military exercises before the city walls. The following year, following a renewed Egyptian rejection of the terms offered for a compromise, the fleet of Great Britain bombarded the city, and a British expeditionary force was sent into Syria. In short, the Egyptians were forced to abandon the entire region; in compensation, they were recognized to be free of the Ottoman Empire.

Caiphas, looking towards Mount Carmel.
Apl. 24th 1839

Haifa, looking towards Mount Carmel

Plate 104

24 April 1839

After sketching a few more views of Akko, Roberts set out for Mt. Carmel, riding along the bayshore. After crossing the riverbed of the Kishon, made famous by the song of Deborah and Barak, he reached the port of Haifa, where he was forbidden to enter as soon as he announced that he was arriving from the south. A new epidemic of the plague had in fact broken out near Jaffa. The Englishman, nevertheless, halted long enough to sketch an overall view of the city, including himself in the sketch, shown drawing while dressed in Eastern clothing. The earliest documentation of the city that we have dates from the fourth century B.C., but throughout antiquity and during the Arab occupation it was a place of no particular importance. It was not until the town was conquered by the Crusaders that it began to develop as the port of the Frankish kingdom of Palestine, with the name of Caiphas. It was destroyed in 1191 by Saladin, and it remained a humble village until the eighteenth century, when it was entirely rebuilt.

The port expanded rapidly and gained in importance during the nineteenth century. Today Haifa is the most important commercial port and destination for tourists in Israel. Here all of the products of the Jezreel Valley are brought, from an area that was once a marsh and is now the breadbasket for the entire region. The urban fabric from the trading sections of the port climbs the slopes of Mt. Carmel, luxuriant with sumptuous gardens from which one can look out over the bay as far as Akko and to the hills of Lebanon beyond. The convent that stands atop Mt. Carmel, clearly visible in this illustration, is probably where the name of the famous order of the Carmelite friars originated. Roberts was received there with great kindness and courtesy. The monks showed him, among other things the chapel, then unfinished, which was being built over the cavern in which the vision of the Virgin appeared to Elijah. After sharing a pleasant meal with his newfound friends, Roberts left the monastery at sunset and rode four hours by moonlight, and then camped for the night.

From David Roberts's journal:

April 24th - We passed on, and ascended Mount Carmel, where we were received with great kindness by the monks. They showed us the chapel, still unfinished, which, they say, covers the cave in which Elijah saw a vision of the Holy Virgin. The design is Italian, and very elegant. We saw also a statue of Elijah trampling on the priests of Baal, but they were proudest of a Virgin and Child, just received from Genoa. We ascended the belfry, from which the scene is very fine...

THE RUINS OF AN IONIC TEMPLE

Plate 105

25th-26th April 1839

*A*n insistent and unfortunate rain forced the entire company to spend the better part of the 25th of April in their tents; in the afternoon, after making a short distance, Roberts decided to set up camp near a fountain dating from Roman times. The following morning, the caravan passed by a small village, called Nakhura, and began to follow an ancient Roman road, which for many stretches appeared still to be in excellent condition. At the peak of a slight rise, the Englishman clear sign that the complex had been razed to the ground by one of the earthquakes that were so frequent in the area. In this connection, the artist was put out to note that neither these noble ruins nor the city that must in all likelihood have stood around the temple had a name, and that for long years they had lain in undeserved oblivion. Fragments of sculptures and the rubble of walls lay scattered over an enormous expanse of ground, now covered in part by sand dunes and patches of

Ruins called Om. El Hamed near Tyr

ran into the ruins of a great Greek temple, the front of which must have measured one hundred ninety-seven feet across, while the depth was probably double, in obediance to the most typical classical standards. Shafts of columns and Ionic capitals, in an excellent state of preservation, were tumbled in great confusion with other, Doric columns, a vegetation. Roberts conjectured that these might have been the last vestiges of a city founded by Alexander the Great.
Even the surrounding region appeared to have been intensely cultivated long ago.
Leaving the ruins of the temple behind them, the travellers set out again along the road to Tyre, and they were soon within sight of Cape Blanco.

April 25th 1839.

David Roberts R.A.

From David Robert's journal:

April 26th - On a height we found the remains of an extensive Greek temple... This building must have been at least 400 feet in length, and 200 feet in depth, and it is singular as it has passed unnoticed...

CAPE BLANCO

Plate 106

26th April 1839

In the early hours of the afternoon of the 26th of April, Roberts and his travelling companions began to climb the daunting trail cut into the sheer cliff walls of Cape Blanco, also known as Ras-el-Abiad. A lowering sky hemmed in the horizon, while huge storm clouds gathered around the promontory; from far below came the dull muttering of waves breaking against the shoals, several hundred feet beneath. The steep little track was made even more perilous now and again by avalanches and landslides, and a low wall of teetering rocks was the only safeguard between the wayfarer and the void. The trail wound its way over rocks worn low by the passage of thousands of caravans and countless carts; two deep tracks had been worn into the yielding limestone. The promontory was completely exposed to the western winds, and received the direct blast of storms blowing in from the open Mediterranean; heavy seas struck at the unprotected base of the promontory, driving the spray straight up and dousing even the steep mule track. Under ordinary conditions, Cape Blanco is certainly one of the most charming sites on the entire Lebanese coast, but on the day David Roberts visited there, the spectacle provided by the unbridled forces of nature cast a sort of spell, and the artist became determined to stay as long as was required to sketch the remarkable scene.

Climbing down the northern slope of Cape Blanco, the travellers soon reached the Phoenician plain and came to the springs called the Wells of Solomon, the waters of which were used to drive numerous waterwheels, and then to feed the aqueduct leading to the nearby city of Tyre.

TYRE, SEEN FROM THE ISTHMUS

Plate 107

*P*assing the Wells of Solomon, after roughly an hour's hike, the travellers came to the ancient city of Tyre. As they approached the site, the remains of the Phoenician city became clearer to the eye, particularly in those areas where the wind had swept away the sand. The glorious metropolis of bygone millennia had been reduced to little more than a humble collection of houses. The mosque in the town appeared to Roberts to be so tattered and shabby that he felt that the ancient prophecy - that the mosque would one day be transformed into a boulder upon which the fishermen would stretch their nets to dry - must already have come true.
The houses were in relatively good condition, however, and the streets were reasonably clean. A few ships rode at anchor in the port, but the city that had once settled colonies across the vast expanse of the Mediterranean was no more than a shadow of her former self, reduced to a petty trade in tobacco, lumber, and coal.
The population had shrunk to just three thousand, and the town was huddled at the tip of the promontory, while the urban settlement on the mainland had long ago been completely abandoned. The town's supply of fresh water was amply provided by two springs that bubbled forth not far from the sea, but which were believed to be linked in some way - by some

conduit running under the isthmus - to the springs of Ras-el-Ain, an hour's march away in the plain. The sole surviving ruins of the city on the mainland lay hidden under the dunes, or else had been incorporated into the breakwater that was said to have been built by Alexander the Great during the siege, and which turned the island of Tyre into a peninsula.

In this illustration by Roberts, we can clearly see, to the left, the main port and the tower that stood near the two fountains; on the opposite side, one can see the ruins of the Christian cathedral. The tower in the foreground was connected to the island by the ruins of a stone wall, and may once have formed part of a fortified complex built by the Saracens.

From David Roberts's journal:

April 26th - By-and-bye we approached the fountains called the Wells of Solomon, the water from which drives a number of mills, besides supplying the aqueduct for the use of Tyre. Another hour's ride along the sands brought us in front of ancient Tyre...

26th April 1839

THE PORT OF TYRE

Plate 108

27th April 1839

*A*ccording to linguists, the modern name of Tyre - Sur - in the Semitic dialect spoken by the local population of Phoenicians origins, means rock. Today, the same term refers to a fishing village in southern Lebanon. Up until the time of Alexander the Great, the promontory upon which the modern city now stands was still made up of two islands, and was separated from the mainland by a narrow stretch of sea; in time, accumulations of sand turned this into an isthmus. Prior to the tenth century B.C., the larger island was the site of the city proper, with the port and the merchant's quarter, while on the smaller, southern island, stood a temple consecrated to a divinity which the Greeks associated with Olympian Zeus. Hiram I, King of Tyre, at last decided to join the two islands with a Cyclopean masonry; over the centuries that followed, the northern basin was enclosed with a massive breakwater, which traced a curve that ran parallel with the island's coastline. The imposing remains of this barrier, which can still be seen, just breaking the surface of the sea, are clearly shown in this illustration by Roberts, who wrote that he had been able to glimpse, at the base of the underwater wall, fragments of huge marble or stone pillars, arrayed regularly side by side; these remarkable foundation stones, which may have been made with material taken from other constructions, can be clearly seen in the plate, almost at the center of the scene.

From David Roberts's journal:

April 27th - Made some sketches. Found a ruinous tower of Saracenic construction - the stones of great size, with foundations of similar structures stretching across the isthmus, jutting into the sea.

David Roberts R.A.

Tyr... ancient Tyre... april 27th 1839.

GENERAL VIEW OF TYRE

Plate 109

27th April 1839

Founded roughly in 2800 B.C. by the Phoenicians, Tyre was for many years under the rule of the pharaohs of Egypt. It won back its independence during the reign of Rameses II, and then enjoyed a period of great prosperity. Tyre was, in fact, a city of great craftsmen who, with remarkable skill, practiced the arts of metallurgy, dyeing with the color purple, weaving, and glass manufacture. Their trade in these products extended throughout the Mediterranean, all the way into Spain and northwestern Africa, where many colonies were founded; some of these colonies later became powerful states in their own right. By the end of the eighth century B.C., Tyre was taken by the Assyrians. Though under foreign rule, the memory of the city's history and the advantages of being left politically unfettered led repeatedly to wholesale attempts at rebellion. These efforts were quashed with equal persistence, however. In the years that followed, Tyre paid tribute to Egypt, and then to the Babylonian Empire. In the wake of the decline of Babylonia, Tyre fell prey in A.D. 538 to Emperor Cyrus. The Persian ruler showed clemency and offered the city considerable freedom, thus ensuring that he was paid absolute allegiance. This was a major factor in the resistance Tyre made to the siege of Alexander the Great, who finally took the town. Once the Macedonian general died, Tyre was long fought over by the Lagids and the Seleucids. In the end, it was annexed by the Romans in 64 B.C., yet even under the Empire, it maintained its standing as a free city, though its times of great prosperity were in fact long over. In A.D. 335, it was the site of a Christian synod, and later it was handed over from Byzantine domination to Arab rule. It was then assaulted and taken by the Crusaders in 1124. Some one hundred-sixty years later the town was recaptured by Muslims who, worried that the position was tactically untenable, preferred to destroy it. Tyre was partially rebuilt over the centuries that followed, but it certainly never again attained its long-lost splendor.

SAREPTA

Plate 110

Sarepta. April 27th, 1839.

*S*etting out from the city of Tyre around eleven o'clock in the morning, Roberts and his fellow travellers continued along their way northwards, skirting the coast. After a while, they descried on the horizon what must surely be the monumental remains of a great city of the past, which they soon discovered was the noble Sarepta. Mentioned in both the Old Testament and the New Testament, the city enjoyed periods of great prosperity, under the Roman Empire and later under Arab domination; it was elevated to a bishopric during the Crusades, and in the twelfth century it was fortified and a new port was built. Later, because of the frequent Saracen raids, the coastal area was progressively abandoned, and the population took refuge inland, on a hill, where the village of Surafend now stands. Not far from the village, toward the sea, Roberts noticed a small mosque, supposedly built on the site of the house where the prophet Elias was believed to have found shelter, and where the prophet brought the widow's son back to life with prayer. In this illustration, which depicts the area surrounding the ancient Sarepta, the scenery is as different as can be from that of the earlier views of southern Palestine. The highlands have a sharper profile, and the chain of the Lebanon Mountains, covered with snow, appears on the horizon.

From David Roberts's journal:

April 27th - Leaving Tyre at 11A.M.,
we came upon the remains of what
must have been a large town, with two
beautiful little bays. The hill behind is
perforated with caves.

27th April 1839

252

SIDON. Looking Towards LEBANON

VIEW OF SIDON, TOWARDS LEBANON

Plate 111

27th April 1839

*S*idon can be seen on the horizon just a short way from the ruins of Sarepta, but the travellers were caught by nightfall long before they had attained their destination that day. To make things worse, a platoon of guards stopped them outside the city and ordered them to show their health certificates, since they had received word of the epidemic that swept through Palestine. Neither Roberts nor any of his travelling companions possessed any such documents; the irate Englishman made the guards understand however that he possessed a safe-conduct, given him personally by Mohammed Ali Pasha. He told them that if they continued to hinder his passage there would certainly be unpleasant consequences on the following day, as soon as he was able to inform the governor of Sidon. These words had the desired effect, and one of the guards was assigned to accompany them to a place on the beach, just south of the town. By the time they reached the beach, they were weary and worn, but to their surprise a wind storm sprang up, and it was only through the greatest of efforts that they finally succeeded in pitching their tents. Although the illustration reproduced here does not depict the episode in question, of the four plates devoted to Sidon, it certainly best describes the city as Roberts saw it, with the mountains of Lebanon in the background and the broad bay looking out to the Mediterranean.

SIDON, SEEN FROM THE SOUTH

Plate 112

28th April 1839

*T*he escorting guard who had spent the night in the encampment on the beach conducted the Englishman and his travelling companions into the city on the 28th of April, making way for them everywhere they went and calling incessantly upon the crowd to let them pass, warning all those passing or still present that their companions were still under quarantine.

In his journal, Roberts noted that Sidon certainly enjoyed an enchanting location, perched as it was atop a high promontory overlooking the sea and boasting a stout and well-protected harbor. The city's hinterland was fertile and well cultivated; the olive groves were numerous, as was the case throughout Syria. Everywhere orange groves and vineyards alternated with fig trees and pomegranate trees. Long rows of mulberry bushes indicated that the silkworm breeding industry was quite prosperous. The city itself gave off a sense of tranquil prosperity, with clean and solidly built houses, wide streets, and well-dressed, healthy citizens.

The sole defect was the general absence of any worthy relics of the past. In fact, during his rapid tour of the city, Roberts noted only a few granite columns lying headlong in the dust and some mosaic floors. The small building that stands in the foreground in this illustration was venerated by Jews as well as Christians and Muslims as the Tomb of Zebulon, one of the ten sons of Jacob, and founder and namesake of one of the Tribes of Israel.

255

The Citadel of Sidon

Plate 113

28th April 1839

Despite the many difficulties besetting him, Roberts was quite determined to make a few sketches of the city, and one of the subjects that interested him greatly was the Citadel, a massive structure built out into the sea a few yards off the beach, connected to terra firma by a solid bridge made of stone blocks. Today, the entire fortified complex lies in almost total ruins, but at Roberts's time it was still in fairly good condition.

Although this plate clearly shows a number of features without a doubt, and in all likelihood, from the time of St. Louis, who was also King Louis IX of France. Along a coastline that is notoriously scanty in good harbors and that is often swept by insidious and even violent winds, the presence of a port as safe and advantageous as Sidon was practically a title to active trade and great prosperity.

The possession of this town, therefore, was of crucial strategic importance, and was well worth the effort of establishing secure military

typical of Islamic architecture, such as the low central dome and the lobed arch on the right side of the structure, the foundation of the fortress dates back to the Crusades, defenses. This explains why the Muslims, as soon as they took the city, immediately set about restoring the Crusaders' Citadel, adopting it as their stronghold.

From David Roberts's journal:

28th April, Sunday - ... I got one or two splendid views of an ancient fort, connected with the land by a bridge of several arches. The houses of Sidon seem large, but I could discover few antiquities...

SIDON

Plate 114

28th April 1839

The earliest documentation of the name Sidon appears in a number of Egyptian documents dating from the thirteenth century B.C. Governed by kings, like other Phoenician cities, Sidon skillfully maneuvered amidst the struggles between Egypt, Babylonia, and the Hittites; meanwhile it prospered greatly on the trade between the Near East and the Mediterranean basin. After Sidon fell under the domination of Nineveh, it was caught up in the struggle against the Assyrians. The latter destroyed the city in 675 B.C. When the city rose once again to renewed splendor, it first became a vassal of the Egyptians, then fell into the hands of the Babylonians, and lastly came under Persian rule. The Persians razed Sidon, but in time the city was rebuilt and, in 332 B.C. it surrendered willingly to Alexander the Great. Following the premature death of the great conqueror, the city became a vassal of first the Lagid and later the Seleucid sovereigns. In 64 B.C., it finally fell to the Romans. In ancient times, Sidon, now called Saida, had always been a city of great traders and great manufacturers. The city's merchants and businessmen sailed their ships to every port on the Mediterranean, and even ventured beyond the strait of Gibraltar, plying the Atlantic coast of Europe all the way up to Brittany and down along the shores of Africa. The colonization carried out by this Phoenician city is documented by a number of coins dating from the fifth and the sixth centuries B.C. Upon these coins, it is possible to read: "Sidon, mother of Carthage, Hippona, Cithius, Tyre." The inhabitants of ancient Sidon are also credited with having transformed the hieroglyphic system of writing practiced by the Egyptians into a purely phonetic - and hence alphabetic - system of writing, the true ancestor of modern writing. In the earliest years of Christianity, Sidon was certainly given the status of an episcopal see, and the earliest name of a bishop of Sidon that appears in an official document is that of Theodore, who in A.D. 325 took part in the First Council of Nicaea. During the Crusades, Sidon was at first ignored by the knights of Christendom, but its highly strategic location made it essential for them to take it. Sidon was repeatedly besieged by Baldwin I, the new king of Jerusalem, and it finally fell in 1111. Saladin retook it and restored it to Muslim rule, and the city changed hands again and again, undergoing bloody destruction each time that it did so. Once it had definitively become an Islamic possession, Sidon enjoyed in the seventeenth century a new period of splendor due to the tireless labors of the Druse Emir Fakhr-el-Din, who embellished the city with magnificent palaces. As the port of Beirut gradually grew in prosperity and influence, the port of Sidon, experienced an equally rapid decline. Still Sidon conserved its opulence and the appearance of sober dignity that Roberts had an opportunity to appreciate so thoroughly.

259

ARRIVAL IN BAALBEC

Plate 115

On the same day that he reached Sidon, where his stay was necessarily quite brief due to the problems mentioned above, Roberts set off once again in the direction of the fabled Baalbec. After a stretch of coastline, the small group of travellers began to climb an extension of the Mountains of Lebanon. At the peak, they camped for the night. The next day was spent crossing the difficult and tiring coastal chain, though the obstacles of the trip were in part offset by the remarkable beauty of the natural setting. The old Roman road ran through the territory of the Druse, a people that belonged to a sect of the Muslim religion. That evening, the English artist confided to the pages of his diary that, since it had been impossible to replenish their supplies at Sidon, they were running dangerously short on foodstuffs. They were completely out of tea, wine, and alcohol, they still had a little coffee but no sugar at all, and they had used up all their fuel oil. The only consolation they could afford before lying down to sleep at night was a pipeful of tobacco. On the morning of the 30th of April, the group of travellers found itself in the region inhabited by the Maronites, a local community of Christians that had preserved its independence over the course of many centuries - the fields here appeared luxuriant and well-kept, and the people were healthy and cheerful. The earliest light of dawn on the 1st of May caught the travellers between the mountains of Lebanon and those of the Antilebanon. By noon they had reached a mountain town called Ab Elias and, by afternoon, the provincial capital, Zahleh. There, as they were taking on supplies, Roberts was told that an insurrection was under way in Baalbec. In the most martial manner he could muster, Roberts requested an audience with the sheik of the city, and showed him his safe-conduct. The governor explained that the revolt had not yet actually broken out, but that it was expected from one moment to the next. He therefore ensured Roberts of his personal support and gave him an escort of three armed men.

At last, on the 2nd of May, Roberts came within sight of Baalbec, where he set up camp in a torrential rain.
The thunderstorms continued all night long, so that by morning Roberts's tent had almost been battered down; the artist had an incipient fever and he was compelled to stay in bed the whole following day.

29th April-3rd May 1839

BAALBEC, THE ANCIENT HELIOPOLIS

Plate 116

4th–5th May 1839

The origins and the earliest history of Baalbec are lost in obscurity. Only the name indicates a clear relationship with the god Baal and, indeed, signifies "City of Baal." It would seem, however, that the original religions of the Syrian city must have been that of Hadad, a god that was, during Hellenistic times, identified with the sun and later with Zeus. From that point onward, the town was called Heliopolis, or "City of the Sun." The cult of Heliopolitan Jupiter, whose earliest relics date from Roman times, would seem to be the result of a far more ancient transposition of religious trappings. Heliopolis is mentioned by the historian Flavius Josephus in connection with his account of the expedition of Pompey that took place in 64 B.C., as well as by Strabo. It became a Roman colony and military base at the beginning of the first century A.D., probably under Augustus, and was called Julia Augusta Felix Heliopolitana - its religious importance was recognized and even fostered by the Romans in the context of their policy at the time of friendly encouragement of neighboring religions. Because of its location, the city was not an important trading center, nor was it situated along fundamental arteries of commerce. The renown of the sanctuary of Heliopolitan Jupiter is documented by the spread of its cult to various regions of the Empire. Trajan himself, just prior to his expedition against the Parthians, in A.D. 115, supposedly consulted the oracle. The importance of the city remained quite considerable until the first half of the third century A.D. and is documented by a great many inscriptions and coins. Under Constantine and Theodosius, the city's temples were converted into Christian churches, and later became an episcopal see. Many events subsequently reduced the city to ruins and rubble: The invasion of the Arabs beginning in A.D. 634; the Crusades that transformed the temples into fortresses; the conquest by Saladin; the plunder by Tamerlane; and the earthquakes of 1664 and 1750. The earliest reports of the ruins of Baalbec came from Martin Baumgarten who visited the site in 1508. But it was not until the beginning of the nineteenth century that the ancient sanctuary city became the destination of men and women of letters and scholars. The first restoration was begun in 1870 and work was resumed with even greater fervor following the visit of the Emperor Wilhelm II. An immense and thorough task of research and published documentation was carried on first by Wiegand and later, by the French school of archeology. The modern city, located in a fertile plain at the foot of the Antilebanon, occupies only a part of the original city plan.

Lesser Temple of Baalbec   May 5th 1839
Looking towards Mount Lebanon

From David Roberts's journal:

4th - Have begun my studies of the temple, of the magnificence of which it is impossible to convey any idea, either by pencil or pen. The beauty of its form, the exquisite richness of its ornament, and the vast magnitude of its dimensions, are altogether unparalleled...
The capitals (Corinthian) are of the most exquisite proportion, and, with the ornamentation of the frieze and cornice, are so deeply and boldly cut, that I should think they must have been carved after being erected.

263

THE SANCTUARY OF BAALBEC

Plate 117

4th–5th May 1839

The western section of the city was largely occupied by the ruins of the great sanctuary of the triad of Heliopolis. These ruins constitute one of the most imposing architectural complexes of all antiquity to have survived in modern times. The giant structure dominated the city's skyline, even though it had been built in the plain, and it was overtopped only by the nearby hill of the Acropolis. The main temple, which was consecrated to Jupiter-Hadad, was made up of four sections arranged along an axis running from east to west. The propylaea along the frontal portico consisted of twelve columns and led into a great hexagonal vestibule some one hundred and ninety-seven feet in width surrounded, in turn, by columns. This space, the walls of which were adorned by niches, formed an intermediate feature, enclosed and self-contained, that served as a passage to the great courtyard standing before the temple proper. The courtyard was four hundred and forty-three feet in length and about three hundred and seventy feet in width. The courtyard was bounded on three sides by porticoes and exedrae, whose monolithic columns made of pink granite can now be seen in the Mosque of Baalbec. At the center of the courtyard stood a great altar in the shape of a four-story tower, with the terrace accessible through an interior stairway.

The temple was two hundred and ninety-five feet in length and one hundred and seventy-seven feet in width. A peripteral Corinthian construction with ten columns along the short sides and nineteen along the longer sides, it stood upon a giant podium that measured forty-six feet high. Of this remarkable structure, only six columns remain standing along the southern side, some ninety-two feet in height; many of the bases of the other columns are still in place. All around, the colossal ruins of the cella can be seen, with fragments of columns and trabeations.

The construction of the great sanctuary must have gone on for several centuries. In the past, it was believed that Antoninus Pius had the temple built, but it has since been determined that the great terrace of the temple dates from the beginning of the first century A.D., and that the temple itself dates from around A.D. 60, while the propylaea probably date from around the time of Septimius Severus. The hexagonal courtyard dates from around the middle of the third century A.D.

Baalbec.

THE CIRCULAR TEMPLE AT BAALBEC

Plate 118

5th May 1839

This illustration portrays one of the architectural wonders of the ancient world: the Temple of Venus. Located near the great temple along the decuman - the principal road of the city - the temple is a small circular and peripteral building with six smooth Corinthian columns, set on a tall podium, and connected to the cella by five indented arcs of a circle. Before the cella, with an interior diameter of just under thirty feet, stands a tetrastile pronaos and a stairway of about twenty steps. Externally, the wall of the cella presents four niches, doubled on the inside and on two superimposed orders. The entire, remarkably elegant structure was probably covered by a small cupola.

This little temple, dedicated to Tyche or to Venus Atargatis, was lavishly decorated with high-relief friezes and statues. Of those, only the bases in the niches still survive. This illustration bears the date of the 5th of May; the same day on which a small mishap befell Roberts that was to have unforeseen consequences: early that morning a servant came to tell him that the mules of his expedition had been requisitioned for the transport of grain to feed the troops. The Englishman lost no time and immediately hastened to the residence of the local governor. The governor, reclining upon his divan, was surrounded by one of the most remarkable and picturesque courts that Roberts had seen in all his years. None of the individuals present wore the same outfit; two richly dressed Beduin chiefs in particular stood out for their sartorial splendor. Groups of attendants bustled here and there. Glittering threads and exquisite clothing could be seen everywhere, and the scene was as colorful as could be. The Englishman was invited to sit at the left hand of the lord of the house, and was able to display his safe-conduct pass only after he had been served coffee. To his enormous surprise no one gave the document a second glance as it was written in Turkish. Nonetheless, they did recognize the signature of Pasha Abbas, and the governor apologized for the misunderstanding. He gave the order to return the animals to Roberts immediately. Roberts then expressed the desire to visit Damascus, which was only a two-day ride away. The high official immediately offered him an escort soldier and a letter of presentation to the governor of that city.

267

THE EASTERN PORTICO OF THE TEMPLE OF BACCHUS

Plate 119

To the south of the Great Temple, oriented in the same direction and in a far superior state of conservation, is the Small Temple, also said to be a temple of Bacchus. This is a peripteral building (i.e., surrounded by a single row of columns), with eight columns on each facade and fifteen columns on the longer sides, and has an elongated plan. The podium upon which the temple stands is just about sixteen feet tall, and before it is a stairway with thirty-four steps. On the interior, the cella, which is roughly almost sixty feet high, is punctuated by elegant Corinthian half-columns which frame a double order of niches. The ornamental details, particularly abundant in the portal and in the trabeation, are marked by a style quite similar to that found in the courtyard of the great sanctuary. The building, which is still imposing in appearance despite the extensive decrepitude, dates from about the middle of the second century A.D. The attribution to Bacchus was made based upon the reliefs, many of which portray racemes of grape vines. It is believed however that the temple was also dedicated to the triad of Heliopolis, and more specifically to Mercury, the Roman personification of the local deity Shamash. The main temple would thus be dedicated to the official cult, while the smaller one would be dedicated to the mystery rites. Roberts was greatly impressed by the spectacle of the colossal ruins of Baalbec, whose magnificence in his eyes transcended any possible description. Although he was feverish, the beauty of the temples, the exquisite richness of the friezes, the incomparable proportions of the entire complex worked so overpowering an enchantment upon him that he spent four days wandering through the ruins, sketching frantically, and noting sizes and proportions in his notebook. In this plate, in particular, it is possible to grasp the truly astonishing proportions of the Temple of Bacchus; the view of the eastern portico clearly shows the refined craftsmanship of the Corinthian capitals and of the cornices.

THE DOORWAY OF THE
TEMPLE OF BACCHUS

Plate 120

8th May 1839

The great doorway of the temple of Bacchus was one of the pieces of architecture that most stimulated Roberts's artistic sensibilities during his stay at Baalbec. The Englishman was not only impressed with the remarkable quality of the friezes, but also by the colossal proportions of the structure. Although the architrave had been seriously damaged by an earthquake, and the central portion was dangling in a precarious state of equilibrium, the sober elegance of the whole seemed to Roberts to be a work of incomparable beauty. The racemes and the interwoven acanthus leaves were exquisite in style, and suggested a lightness of touch that contrasted sharply with the majestic eagle, its wings spread wide, that was carved upon the lower side of the architrave. Roberts had promised himself that he would complete at least seven drawings of the ruins of Baalbec, and it is worth noting that he was elected a member of the Royal Academy, thanks to the oil-on-canvas painting upon his return to London, based upon the sketch of the great portal. Unfortunately, the stay at Baalbec was troubled by an increasingly troublesome fever, and at last the artist was forced to abandon his plans of continuing to visit Damascus and Palmyra and indeed convinced him to set out in the

direction of Beirut, though with great misgivings. Setting out on the morning of the 8th of May, he crossed once again the mountains of Lebanon, and within days he was in sight of the great port city. In Beirut, he met up again with John Kinnear and a number of other friends, happily spending time with them and telling of his recent adventures. On the 13th of May he boarded a ship bound for Alexandria, where he arrived after a voyage of three days.

He then continued his voyage, reaching Malta, where he was obliged to spend three weeks in quarantine. Then a five-day voyage aboard the steamer "Volcano" took him to Gibraltar; after spending a week in Cadiz, as a guest of the consul, who was a friend of long acquaintance, and after a few more days in Lisbon, David Roberts finally returned to London, docking on the 21st of July, after an absence of eleven months.